COLS
WRIGHT STATE UNIVERSITY
UNIVERSITY LIBRARY
0 00 13 0154171 8

PRACTICAL STRATEGIES FOR TAMING THE PAPER AND PEOPLE PROBLEMS IN TEACHING

PRACTICAL STRATEGIES FOR TAMING THE PAPER AND PEOPLE PROBLEMS IN TEACHING

By

ANNE WESCOTT DODD, M.A., C.A.S.

Lecturer in Education
Bates College
Lewiston, Maine
Visiting Lecturer in Education
Colby College
Waterville, Maine

CHARLES C THOMAS • PUBLISHER
Springfield • Illinois • U.S.A.

Published and Distributed Throughout the World by

CHARLES C THOMAS • PUBLISHER
2600 South First Street
Springfield, Illinois 62794-9265

ISBN 0-398-05386-3

Library of Congress Catalog Card Number: 87-12525

With THOMAS BOOKS *careful attention is given to all details of manufacturing and design. It is the Publisher's desire to present books that are satisfactory as to their physical qualities and artistic possibilities and appropriate for their particular use.* THOMAS BOOKS *will be true to those laws of quality that assure a good name and good will.*

Printed in the United States of America
Q-R-3

Library of Congress Cataloging in Publication Data

Dodd, Anne W.
Practical strategies for taming the paper and people problems in teaching / by Anne Wescott Dodd.
p. cm.
Bibliography: p.
Includes index.
ISBN 0-398-05386-3
1. Classroom management. 2. Teachers—Time management.
3. Records—Management. I. Title.
LB3013.D62 1987 87-12525
371.1'02—dc19 CIP

To Felicia Ferrara Wescott,
Archie H. Wescott,
and James H. Dodd
with love and appreciation
for taming me.

PREFACE

MY FIRST YEAR of teaching was a disaster for which I was not prepared and from which there was no relief but time and experience. After several years as a teacher in Southern California and Maine at six junior and senior high schools, I learned how to cope with the complex demands. I stopped thinking about changing careers because I couldn't imagine any other job which would be so challenging and rewarding.

Later as a senior high school assistant principal and middle-school principal and more recently as a college teacher of students who plan to become teachers, I had to examine the methods and strategies I discovered (most of which had become almost instinctive behavior after so many years) so that I could explain them to the teachers and student teachers under my supervision. In this book I've put all these ideas together in order to help beginning teachers who are struggling to survive as I once did, teachers-to-be who soon will be, and experienced teachers who continue to look for new ways to deal with old problems.

When I actually began writing the book, I discovered that many of the methods I had found so successful in dealing with people and problems were integrated into my whole philosophy of teaching and learning, but other teachers can adopt or adapt most of them to make their own jobs easier.

Teaching is somewhat like taming lions. And the lions come in many forms: too much paper, too many meetings, the disruptive student, the angry parent, the demanding administrator. What they have in common is that at any time they can, individually or collectively, so overwhelm teachers that their ability to do the job or do it well is impaired. This book is about taming these lions. It will show teachers how to control and cope with the demands and problems they face on the job.

But there's another more important, through less obvious, aspect of taming the lions, which is important for teachers to realize and which will be familiar to readers of Antoine de Saint-Exupéry's *The Little Prince.* When the fox meets the little prince, he tells him, "I cannot play with you because I am not tamed." Because the little prince doesn't understand what he means, the fox explains that "taming" is an act too often neglected and adds, "It means to establish ties." According to the fox, "One only understands the things one tames," and taming requires time and patience. Once the little prince tames the fox, however, the fox will no longer be just a fox like a hundred thousand other foxes. He will be unique.

The best teachers don't limit themselves to dealing with facts and figures, policies and procedures, homework papers and unit tests, because they understand that motivating students, helping them stretch and grow intellectually, requires the time, patience, and care that it takes to establish ties with individual students. Although the fox doesn't have teaching in mind when he shares his secret with the little prince, his words certainly apply: "What is essential is invisible to the eye." The best teachers, the ones who foster a lifelong love for learning and really make a difference in students' lives, want very much to teach but also to tame their lions in this special way.

Even though this book appears to focus only on the nuts and bolts of teaching, I hope that readers will look beyond the printed lines and see that what is essential in teaching and taming is invisible to the eye.

A.W.D.
Brunswick, Maine

INTRODUCTION

TEACHING IS tough. Every day the paper demands and people problems you encounter proliferate like so many lions that need to be tamed.

You spend a sunny Sunday grading papers and planning the week's work for your classes and come in Monday ready to begin a productive week. You head for the ditto machine to run off copies of the unit test. No paper. You finally find the custodian who gets paper for you. Later in your room you rush to staple the tests, sort out the forms and notices you found in your box to pass out to homeroom students, and write the assignments on the board. Already you feel the pressure building.

The bell rings. The students are everywhere, noisily reliving the weekend. Five minutes to take attendance, get a lunch count, read the daily bulletin, and pass out those papers to students—overdue notices from the library, appointments with guidance, flyers about the school fair, and notices outlining the sign-up procedure for the next year's courses. The bell rings before you get to the last announcement. Homeroom students rush out, bumping the period one students on their way in.

Getting students started on the unit test takes longer than you anticipated. Five students are absent. Johnny brings a note from his mom, asking that you give him an extra day to study for the test because they had company all weekend and the dog almost choked to death on a bone. (She doesn't mention the overdue assignments about which you wrote her two weeks ago.) Susie has to tell you about the darling kittens her cat just had. (No, you really can't take one.) You are still sorting papers on your desk and eyeballing the room for cheating when the bell rings. Another chaotic scramble as period one students leave, asking what the assignment is (Couldn't they read what you had written on the board?) and complaining that questions two and seven were definitely unfair. Period two students crown around your desk, asking if the test can be postponed while at the same time trying to glimpse the test questions.

And so it goes. You break up a fight between two students at lunch and end up missing most of yours while you explain to the vice-principal what happened. Your prep period is just long enough to take two aspirin, meet with the guidance counselor, and return a phone call to the secretary in the superintendent's office who snippily reminds you that personnel still hasn't received your updated personal information form. After school you stew in silence while the department discusses revising the scope and sequence of the curriculum. When you finally leave, exhausted and tense, you're carrying five sets of unit tests, your grade book, your plan book, and the K-12 curriculum guide. There's no way you can watch that TV special tonight: grades for the semester are due in the office at 2 P.M. tomorrow. You try not to think of the faculty meeting scheduled for later this week, the second semester goals and objectives that your department head and principal expect on Friday, and the parent conferences next week.

Teaching is stressful. There's no magic formula for eliminating the stress, but there are ways to reduce it. The lions that threaten to overpower you can be tamed.

Practical Strategies for Taming the Paper and People Problems in Teaching will show you how to:

- Deal with administrativia more quickly and easily.
- Organize papers, books, and materials so that you can find what you need when you need it.
- Gain some personal benefit from required meetings and non-teaching duties, such as cafeteria supervision.
- Arrange and decorate your classroom to eliminate trivial, time-consuming tasks and to encourage students to become more responsible.
- Plan your time and lessons so that you're free from school responsibilities when you want or need to be.
- Prevent most conflicts with students and solve the few you can't avoid without punishing yourself with after-school detention.
- Lessen the burden of correcting papers and eliminate arguments with students about the grades they receive.
- Motivate students to do their assignments and complete them on time so that you end up failing fewer students.
- Get students to work cooperatively as individuals with you and with their peers in small groups.

- Inform and involve parents and administrators so that they will work with you rather than against you.
- Keep your cool when you feel the tension build.
- Maintain or renew your enthusiasm for teaching even after years on the job.

Once you've tamed the lions, you'll see teaching not as just another way to earn a living but as a challenging and rewarding career.

CONTENTS

PRACTICAL STRATEGIES FOR TAMING THE PAPER AND PEOPLE PROBLEMS IN TEACHING

CHAPTER ONE

ATTACKING ADMINISTRIVIA

"Ms. Sennett, I didn't get your inventory. Do you have it now? It was due two days ago!" The principal waits while Ms. Sennett paws through piles of papers, books, and folders on her desk.

"I'm sorry. It's here somewhere. I just forgot. So many things to do, you know." She hands him the completed form.

"I have things to do myself, Ms. Sennett, and I don't like wasting time this way. See that it doesn't happen again. By the way, don't forget that your budget request is due Friday."

As the principal leaves, Ms. Sennett says to herself, "Now where did I put that form? Maybe I didn't pick one up yet."

SCHOOLS without paperwork and meetings will never exist. Like other bureaucracies, schools couldn't run without them. What seems useless to you may be very necessary to someone else. You can't eliminate the administrivia, so the best approach is to deal with it as quickly and as painlessly as possible.

CALENDAR CONTROL

Begin With a Calendar or Datebook

A calendar or datebook is essential. For teachers one which follows the fiscal or academic year is the most useful. Because your life is measured out in school years, your new year begins in September rather than January. Get a datebook which you can carry in your pocket or purse so you'll always have it with you. It's great for jotting reminders about your personal as well as your professional obligations, but the datebook is useless if you don't have it with you when you need it.

If you get into the habit of making your datebook *the* one place where you list everything you have to do, you'll always have it with you because you won't be able to get along without it.

Copy the School Calendar in Your Datebook

The academic/fiscal year calendars and datebooks are available in the stores in June. They include July of one year through the end of June the next year. When your school district gives you a copy of the next year's school calendar, copy all the dates of marking periods, vacations, holidays, and so forth into your own datebook. (You may want to check the number of days in each quarter. I've found mistakes which were changed when I reported them to the central office. Who knows when someone else would have found them? Correcting a mistake early on is much easier for everyone. I hate to think of the confusion which would have resulted if no one discovered until November that the first quarter was a week longer than it should have been!)

Because your calendar probably shows only a week at a time, also put a note to yourself about a special date a week ahead. For example, if the first quarter ends on the first Friday in November, write a note on the last Friday of October, "First quarter ends next week." While you're planning ahead, record all the birthdays and anniversaries you're supposed to remember in your datebook, too. Since you'll be using the calendar on a regular basis, if you have a note about an upcoming birthday, you won't forget to buy that present.

If you really want to get organized, you might spend a few minutes brainstorming all the things you have to remember to do throughout the year. Write notes in your calendar to remind you when your car needs a new registration or inspection sticker, your driver's license needs renewal, the house taxes or insurance need to be paid, you need to schedule a checkup with the doctor or dentist. This calendar will be your bible for the year, so include as much useful information as you can.

As you will see in Chapter Three, establishing a master calendar is also the first step in managing and reducing your workload when school begins. Anticipating what's coming up in the future that will have some effect on your school plans is the key to making your job easier.

Don't forget to add frequently called phone numbers in the back section of your datebook. One advantage teachers have is the change of pace in the summer. Take a few minutes when you're not so busy to look up the phone numbers you may need and save yourself time when you're overburdened next fall.

REMINDER AND REWARD: THE "TO DO" LIST

You probably have no trouble thinking of a list of things to do as a good way to remind yourself what needs to be done, but have you considered it as a way of rewarding yourself for jobs you've finished? Everyone enjoys a sense of accomplishment, and you can give yourself a psychological lift just by crossing things off a list.

Divide your list into two parts: immediate tasks (small jobs that can or must be completed right away) and long-range projects that you will chip away at over time. If you break the bigger long-range jobs into smaller pieces and add these to your immediate list, you'll get a sense of accomplishment as you go along even though the whole task may not be completed for a couple of weeks.

By using the two-part "to do" list, you'll be visually reminded to think and plan ahead and thereby avoid the stress of facing an overwhelming task all at once at the last minute. For example, by writing "second quarter lesson plans" on your long-range list as soon as the first quarter is underway, you can use spare moments here and there to jot down ideas, collect materials, sketch out plans, and make copies of handouts you'll need. When the first quarter ends, you'll probably have most of the work done and need to schedule only a short time to tie up the loose ends.

I use a separate sheet of memo paper for my "to do" list and clip it to the cover of my calendar (an executive-style book), but you may find it more convenient to write your list right on the calendar itself. I keep adding tasks to the bottom of my list and make a new copy only when the sheet's so filled it's hard to read. Those crossed-off items show me how much I've accomplised and motivate me to work on the others. Sure, it's a psychological game I play with myself, but it works. Once when the supply of ditto paper suddenly vanished right at the beginning of the second semester, I remained cool and calm while other teachers were grumbling, complaining that they couldn't teach without copies of handouts for students. Mine were all ready to pass out because I'd been working ahead and there had been plenty of ditto paper a few weeks earlier when I ran them off.

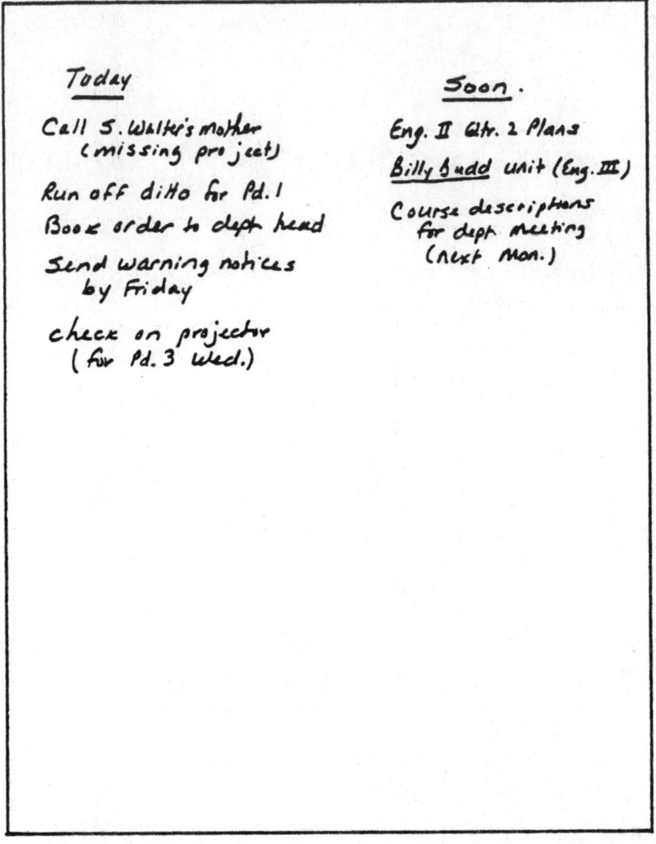

Figure 1. Sample "To Do" list showing what needs to be accomplished today and larger tasks which will be worked on a little at a time until they have been completed.

COMBATTING THE PAPER PLAGUE

(1) USE THE CALENDAR TO GET RID OF PAPER. Nothing drives me crazier than pieces of paper. Notes jotted down about upcoming appointments and memos from the principal about due dates and meeting times clutter up my life. With the calendar you can throw a great deal of paper away. When you get a memo announcing a meeting, record the information in your calendar and put the memo in the circular file. If you have an organized principal, you will get a list of all faculty meetings at the beginning of the year. If so, record all the dates in your calendar immediately and throw the list away.

You'll be amazed at how much paper can be eliminated immediately after you transfer the essential information to your calendar. Do it on a regular basis. Don't allow unnecessary paper to collect.

(2) SAVE STEPS WITH FORMS: FILL THEM OUT FAST. Some of the administrivia comes as forms which you need to fill out. These can't be dispensed with as rapidly as memos which you can read and discard. The key to forms, however, is getting rid of them as soon as possible. If you know the paper has to be filled out, do it right away and get it over with. "Put off until tomorrow what you don't feel like doing today" is not a good rule. Schools being the way they are, chances are you'll have more to fill out tomorrow. If it will take only five minutes to answer the department head's questionnaire, do it now. Get the paper off your desk and the burden off your back. One form to fill out is much easier than two, three, or four facing you all at once. Besides, if you fill the form out and turn it in, you won't have to write a reminder to yourself to do it later, record the due date in your calendar, and find a place to put the paper until you can get to it. You're saving a lot of time by doing the job now.

If you can't take care of a form immediately, tuck it in your calendar where you can't avoid seeing it when you check your schedule for the day. Because it will be in your way, you'll get it done at the first opportunity and it won't get lost or misplaced.

(3) ANTICIPATE INFORMATION YOU'LL NEED AND BE READY FOR FORMS. Many schools request the same information year after year. If you know what will be needed, you can have the information ready. For example, one school in which I taught not only asked for the total enrollment in each class but separate totals for boys and girls as well. It took me a minute or less to record all three figures on the seating chart for each class. When the form arrived as expected, I got the paper completed and out of my hair in seconds. By the way, since enrollments, especially in high school classes, can change from day to day until the add/drop period ends, I record names and enrollment figures in pencil. When a student is added to or dropped from the course, I take a second to change the enrollment figures as I write or erase the student's name.

Filling forms out fast and getting them off your desk will pay off in other ways. The administrators will love you! The fact that you don't hold them up and force them to chase down information they requested but never received will have them singing your praises. The vice-principal may also think twice before assigning *you* to lunch duty or Friday afternoon detention.

(4) HANDLE A PIECE OF PAPER ONLY ONCE. Try to follow this rule always. If the memo or note you get requires a response, respond immediately on the same piece of paper and return it to the sender.

If you skim a memo and it has nothing to do with you, throw it away. What's the point of saving the principal's notice to take care of classroom carpeting when all your classes are in rooms with tiled floors? A word of caution, however: better to skim and discard office memos in the privacy of your classroom. If you are seen in the office glancing at a memo and throwing it away, someone may get the wrong idea. It is a good idea to save time and steps by reading notes as soon as you take them from your box. Some can be taken care of and put in someone else's box while you're right there.

(5) SET UP INDIVIDUAL FILE FOLDERS FOR MEMOS AND MEETING AGENDAS YOU HAVE TO KEEP. Unfortunately, you won't be able to get rid of all the paper that appears in your mailbox or on your desk. After you skim an agenda for an upcoming meeting, for example, note the meeting time and place in your calendar, along with a reminder of anything you personally have to take or do before the meeting. Then file the agenda in the appropriate folder: Faculty Meetings, Curriculum Committee, and so on. So that these folders do not become stuffed with useless, outdated paper, make it your routine to throw away the agenda and other papers you don't need when you file the minutes for that meeting.

Once you get organized, the secret to staying that way is doing little things like filing papers where they belong as soon as you read them and getting rid of every piece of paper you don't need. The job which seems almost effortless when done all the time becomes overwhelming only if you let things pile up. Later in this chapter you'll find tips for managing your files.

(6) DON'T WORRY TOO MUCH ABOUT THROWING PAPER AWAY. Some people hestitate to discard anything because an inner voice warns, "Better not throw that away. You might need it." If that's your problem, remind yourself that someone else will have a copy of the whatever that you can borrow should the need arise. There's probably one person on the faculty who, along with copies of every ditto he's handed out, has also saved every faculty notice and memo for the past twenty years. In the unlikely event you don't know such a person, the school secretary surely has file copies and can help you out.

Be firm with yourself. Only if the piece of paper in question is the one copy in existence should you consider saving it with just a vague feeling that you might need it someday. (I must admit this is easier to say than to do, but every little bit helps!)

(7) USE YOUR BULLETIN BOARD AND WALL FOR GENERAL ANNOUNCEMENTS. Reserve a place on the bulletin board or wall to post

notices of general interest to students, and remember as you add a new one to quickly check for others to throw away.

Get big clips to hold (1) daily or weekly teacher/student bulletins and (2) daily student absence lists. Attach them to the wall in a convenient place near your desk for easy reference. Because you or a student occasionally may need to check backdated bulletins or lists, keep as many of each as the clips will comfortably hold, throwing away a few of the oldest ones as the clip gets full. If you have been stapling or tacking the notices to the bulletin board or keeping them on your desk, consider switching to the clips. Clipping is quicker than stapling or tacking and more reliable than keeping them on your desk because it eliminates the possibility of their getting mixed in with other papers, being carried out of the room, or sliding off into the wastebasket. Also consider delegating the task of posting and clipping notices to a reliable student.

HANDBOOKS, TEACHERS' CONTRACT, AND CURRICULUM GUIDES

Not all of the paper that threatens to bury you comes in single or double sheets. Student and teacher handbooks, the master contract negotiated by the teachers' association, and other school district publications along with their often very overweight cousins, the curriculum guides, shouldn't be filed and forgotten. For your own information and self-protection you should know what they contain. If you're a beginning teacher or a first-year teacher in a new school, skim-read all of these. You can learn a great deal about the school and its procedures and expectations and prevent some future hassles and headaches as well.

It isn't necessary to read everything thoroughly. Focus on the information that will help you now and aim for enough familiarity with the rest so you'll know where to find any information you may have to check back on later.

Student Handbook

Your knowledge of the student handbook is critical to your maintaining the upper hand with students who will try to get around all the rules. To help you remember rules and procedures about such things as what to do about students who are absent from class or late to school, actually write a summary of the rules that affect your dealing with students in the classroom. You're more likely to remember the information if you write it down, and you can easily make a copy of your notes to include in the folder you set up for a substitute teacher.

If you know what the handbook says, you can often avoid arguments or discussions. When a student breaks some rule, simply direct the student to the appropriate section in the handbook and tell him or her to read what it says. You'll also prevent the unpleasant situations that can arise when students know more than the teacher does about the rules. Imagine what can happen when a teacher says, "You see me after school today or else" and the student knows the school policy requires that teachers give students twenty-four hours' notice before keeping them after school.

As you read through the student handbook, take note of the extracurricular activities available to students so that you can, for example, suggest possibilities to a shy student or one who's new to the school. Also, look for activities which interest you. You'll find that one way to improve your relationship with students in your classes is to show interest in their pursuits outside the class. That show-off who's been driving you crazy in period five may completely turn around after you comment on his performance in the school drama production. Because students behave better when they feel you care about them, you can save yourself hours and days of aggravation by spending two fairly pleasant hours at a play or a basketball game. Of course, if you have more time and energy, you can win points from the administration as well as the students by taking on an extracurricular responsibility yourself. In most cases, there's a stipend for the coach or club advisor.

Teacher Handbook

Becoming acquainted with procedures and policies in the teachers' handbook will make routine tasks go more smoothly and also help you avoid unnecessary hassles with administrators.

Find out who has the authority to approve field trip and book purchase requests, how to requisition supplies, where your class exits for fire drills, and which people in the school can answer questions and handle problems in what areas. If you've already been in the school for a while, you know these things, but new teachers can save time by finding out some of these things before school even begins.

The handbook probably also includes obligations and dates which you should note. For example, as part of the evaluation process, you may be required to write a self-assessment by a certain date or supervise an after-school detention at certain times during the year. *Add all of these tasks and dates to your master calendar* along with other important dates, such as dates for the school open house or final evaluation conference. If no specific dates are listed, you can jot the general information down in your calendar at the beginning of the appropriate month, filling in the specific dates as you get them.

Teachers' Master Contract

Except for the current salary schedule, many veteran teachers are often unaware of the provisions in the master contract which the teachers' association has negotiated on their behalf. One teacher, for example, got very angry and blamed the principal for not being able to attend a conference. The unhappy teacher had mentioned the conference to the principal in the hall one morning but never completed the required professional leave form. Naturally, the principal forgot about the conversation so no substitute was hired, and when the teacher reminded the principal about the conference the day before, there was no substitute available. This teacher could have saved himself and the principal a lot of grief if he had checked the professional leave section in the teachers' contract beforehand and followed the procedures described there.

Since the teachers' contract covers teachers' rights and benefits as well as their obligations, the wise teacher realizes that knowing what the contract says is not just a good idea but may often be a matter of self-protection or survival on the job. An administrator, knowingly or unknowingly, may violate the terms of the contract by assigning a teacher too many preparations or too many students, for example. The teacher who's not informed about contract provisions may end up carrying an unnecessarily heavy load.

Curriculum Guides

Unless you teach in a school which has a testing program keyed directly to the curriculum guide, you'll find that these hefty documents which list the skills, concepts, and attitudes students are supposed to master in the various subject areas are used only when teachers are asked to update them, when parents or school board members have questions, or when a school works on a self-study as part of the school accreditation process.

Time spent reading through the curriculum guides to get a general understanding of what the curriculum in your subject area is supposed to be, however, will not be wasted. You'll know what to emphasize in planning lessons, and should a parent or administrator question what you're doing, you'll be on solid ground if you can point to a specific place in the curriculum guide to justify the activity. Of course, it won't hurt your professional image to appear so knowledgeable and professionally responsible.

Because many curriculum guides often suggest activities and methods for teaching various topics, you can glean some good ideas from them. The reminder some bookstores give their customers may apply here: "One good idea will repay the price of this book." The curriculum guide you get for free!

Some school districts have other publications that may be useful. Check them all out just in case. One district I worked in provided new teachers with a handbook which outlined detailed plans for organizing classes during the first week of school. It was worth its weight in gold for inexperienced teachers who had difficulty dealing with all the administrivia, such as checking out textbooks and collecting health information cards, that always comes with the opening of school.

Be sure to file copies of these documents where you can find them. Chances are, when you need to look something up, you'll be in a hurry and won't have time to figure out where they are buried.

FUNCTIONAL FILES

A functional file system is a necessity if you want to save time and energy. All the publications and paper you hang on to are useless if you can't put your fingers on what you need when you need it.

If you're lucky enough to have your own classroom with a file cabinet, you should have plenty of room for the things you want to keep. Don't file anything you won't need for future reference or can easily get from someone else's file should the need arise. Your files won't get overstuffed if you try to follow a simple rule: every time you add something to a folder, check to see if there's something there that you can throw away.

If you don't have a file cabinet to call your own or must travel to several classrooms, invest in a couple of hanging file boxes (available in office supply and some discount stores) or make your own from empty cartons. (The ones that photocopier paper comes in are sturdy and just the right size for letter-sized folders.) I've found the hanging file boxes so accessible and convenient, I've abandoned my file cabinet and set up all my files, one general category to a box, on open shelves. I also discovered that some topics on which I've collected material, such as student assessment and courses I teach, include so many pamphlets and paper that file folders were too small. I've begun using 10″-x-12″ envelope and stationary boxes for these topics. Stacked on a shelf with boldly printed labels on the front, the boxes are readily accessible when I have material to add or retrieve. When I begin a project, I move the whole box on that topic to my desk until the work is finished. This book, for example, has such a box right now. When I quit working for the day, I put everything in the box until next time. Not only does my desk look neat and clean, I also don't have to worry about the manuscript pages getting torn during my cat's nocturnal games.

Another option for storing newsletters, materials for a committee or special projects, or all the notes and handouts you have collected for a specific course or unit is a three-ring binder. Punch holes in the pages and keep everything in order by date or category. Clearly label the binder cover's outside edge before standing it up on your bookshelf. The key here as with the file folders is punching holes and putting items in the appropriate binders as soon as you can and certainly before they get mixed up with other papers on your desk!

Whether you maintain files at school, at home, or in both places, you'll want them organized so that (1) they include all the information you need for later reference and (2) you can find that information quickly and easily. While there are several books and pamphlets available which will tell you how to organize your files using numeric and/or color coding systems, you don't have to set up such a formal system. Make a list of the files you have now (or would create if you are just beginning). Brainstorm other topics for which you should have files. Look at your total list and decide which items can be grouped together under more general headings. Alphabetize the items within each general category.

Master File List

Whatever system you choose, the master file list which shows the names and locations (specific file drawer or box) of all your folders is the key to knowing where everything is. Even if your alphabetization isn't perfect or you have trouble remembering the title you gave a certain file, you'll be able to find files quickly and easily with this master file list.

Type up a list of all the general categories with an alphabetized list of the individual files in each. Double- or triple-space the list so you can pencil in the titles of new files as you create them and keep the list in your desk, in the very front of the top drawer of your file cabinet, or in some other convenient location. When you can't remember where a particular file is located, it's a lot easier and faster to glance at your master list and spot the location than it is to locate it by actually pawing through many folders in the depths of file drawers.

You may want to expand the idea of a master file to cover books and the magazines and journals you save along with their locations. Of course, if you have a computer, you can keep all this information stored there for easy updating, but for quick reference put a hard copy in your desk. As long as you make sure your master list (the index to your files) is up-to-date and you return files promptly after using them, you should be able to find whatever you need very quickly no matter how idiosyncratically you create filing categories.

Categories to Consider for Your Files

Reserve a section or drawer of your file cabinet or an individual file box for each general category. If any general category includes a topic for which you have a large number of individual files, establish a new general category for that topic. If you have a large number of files for college courses you've taken, for example, those files should be considered as a general category rather than as part of your personal file.

Personal File

1. Certification (renewal information and copies of current certificates)
2. Conferences, workshops, and inservice programs attended
3. Contracts and leave requests (employment—your personal copies)
4. Courses taken
5. Evaluations, your copies of forms, such as leave requests
6. Master résumé
7. Recommendation letters (your own)
8. Recommendation letters (written for others)
9. Transcripts
10. Yearly list of students taught and their final grades

General School File

1. Committees, extracurricular activities, general school projects
2. Course description guide (course of study handbook)
3. Curriculum guides
4. Department meetings
5. Faculty meetings
6. Publications (school and district)
7. Student handbook
8. Teachers' contract (negotiated agreement)
9. Teacher handbook

Teaching File

1. Courses you teach—general plans
2. Individual folders for each unit taught with specific plans and resources
3. Handouts—folders containing multiple copies of each

General Reference File

In this category put information and articles you're saving on current trends, issues, and research in education generally and in your curriculum area, as well as other topics which aren't personal or directly connected to the school at which you work or the subjects you currently teach.

Notes on the Personal File

You may prefer to keep your personal file at home because it should contain everything you need to apply for a new job, renew your teaching certificate, check on past or current employment (contracts, evaluations, personal leave requests, and the like), summarize your recent professional development efforts, and write recommendation letters for former students or student teachers.

Maintaining a *master* résumé file is a real time-saver. In addition to a copy of your most recent résumé, collect information which you will use when you update it. Every time you begin serving on a new committee or take on another professional responsibility, jot down the details on a note and drop it into the folder. When you want an up-to-date copy of your résumé in a hurry, everything you'll need to do the job will be right at your fingertips. If you have a computer, store the information on a disk and the job will be completed even faster.

Keeping copies of the *recommendations you've written for others* all in one place can save you a great deal of aggravation and extra work. I got smart after a couple students asked me to write recommendations a year or two after they were in my class. Naturally, I remembered writing letters earlier, but after unsuccessfully searching for those copies, I wasted more time struggling to remember details to write new ones. Now that copies of all those letters go in one place, I only have to make a photocopy, date it, and sign my name. When a narrative response is required to a question on a form, I write my comments so that they make sense when read alone and keep a copy on a blank sheet of paper so that in most cases I can photocopy rather than retype the statement to fulfill future requests from the same students.

The yearly lists of students I teach and their final grades help me remember students I'm asked about when they are no longer in my class. The lists are also handy to get rid of the itch in my head when I just can't remember the name of a particular student although I know just where he sat three years ago!

Saving copies of *recommendations others have written* for me makes it possible for me to apply for a new position and send all the requested information right away without having to bother these busy people again or depend on them (or the university placement bureau where I also have a file) to get the task done in a timely fashion.

Notes on the Teaching File

Organize your teaching file so that you can remove individual folders for long-range and short-term planning. Separate the folders which contain multiple copies of handouts from the resource files which contain general information about courses you teach and those on specific topics or units. There's no point in lugging around a mountain of material when all you need is a small portion of it. Single copies of handouts should be in the resource files, and when you're finished planning a unit, you can check to see how many more copies you'll need to make of the handouts you've used before. If you always put the master ditto or original for photocopying in the same folder with the multiple copies, you'll have no problem making additional copies whenever you need them. Remember that you can use a typewritten original to make ditto masters on a photocopier. Of course, saving the information on a computer disk is even better. Make sure the original is the *bottom* copy in the folder, and consider marking it with a paper clip as well as that you won't accidently hand it to a student.

Notes on the General Reference File

Reserve this space for general information and material you no longer teach but may want to refer to at some later time. Don't be as foolish as I have been several times in the past and assume that you'll never teach a course or unit again. I did, and I was sorry I'd thrown everything away and had to start all over. It will pay, however, to reduce these past files to absolute essentials. It really isn't necessary or practical to save everything.

DESK MANAGEMENT

How much time did you waste last week hunting for something amidst a stack of papers and folders piled up on your desk? A workable file system won't improve your efficiency and effectiveness if you store papers and folders indiscriminately on your desk. All sheets of paper should be filed in the appropriate folders or discarded as soon as you've skimmed them and logged dates and tasks in your calendar or on your "to do" list.

Tips for Organizing Your Desk or Work Area

(1) Gather all the items and supplies you routinely use (dictionary, paper, clips, tape, stapler, etc.) and assign them to specific locations. Get an organizer tray in an office supply store for your top middle drawer and avoid the annoyance of grabbing a rubber band, only to find it stuck to a trail of paper clips which have to be pulled off one by one.

(2) Keep a small memo pad and pen (beside the phone if you have one) so that you can jot down ideas on other topics that occur to you as you work. File these notes in the appropriate folders as soon as you can without interrupting work on your current task.

(3) While many management experts recommend keeping an "in" basket on one side of your desk and an "out" basket on the other, I would suggest you forget the "in" basket altogether if you're the type of person who's apt to use it as a dumping place for things that should be filed elsewhere. The "out" basket should contain only letters, memos, forms, etc. which are ready to go. At the end of the day that basket should be empty.

(4) Get a vertical file holder or reserve a space in your top drawer for those *few* folders you use daily and the ones you need to work on future

projects a little bit at a time. When a project is complete, return the folder to the file.

(5) While you work, keep only the materials you need for that task on your desk top. To decrease the risk of mixing important papers in with others from another file, put everything from one project away before you take out things for another one.

(6) Clear your desk at the end of the day. Leave out only what you'll need first thing in the morning, such as your homeroom folder, for example.

(7) If you find that your daily desk management habits are sloppy, don't despair, but do schedule time once a week to get things back in shape.

(8) Keep personal items, such as photographs and souvenirs, from encroaching on your desktop work space. Consider displaying such items on a wall or bookshelf near your desk so you'll have plenty of elbow room while you work.

TURNING MEETING TIME TO YOUR ADVANTAGE

Like other bureaucratic organizations, schools thrive on meetings. And while meetings can be a way for everyone to share in the decision-making, many are a waste of teachers' valuable time. When you're stuck in a meeting where someone drones on and on about administrative details that could have been written up in a memo, or the same teachers complain about the same problems they griped about last year, figure out ways you can use the time to your advantage. Unless you want to announce your indifference and risk the principal's ire, don't correct papers or knit! But since research shows that experienced teachers are skilled at paying attention to several things at once, you can train yourself to listen to what's being said at the same time you discreetly do something else. In fact, I wrote this poem during a faculty meeting and had it published:

Faculty Meeting*

Words
 words
  words

*Reprinted from *English Journal*, Vol. 60, No. 2. February 1971, p. 214. Published by the National Council Teachers of English.

Trivia now and before and again
Purposeless verbal wandering . . .
meandering . . .
steadily . . .
slowly . . .
humming
Nothing about nothing
continually repeated
continuously repeated
circuitously repeated
Nodding sleepily, I hear
NOTHING!

If writing poems is not your forte, consider the following. As long as you're not noisily shuffling paper around, no one will realize you're doing anything more than taking notes on what's being said.

(1) Brainstorm some possible solutions to some of the age-old problems being discussed. If you come up with an idea that seems workable, discuss it with the principal and your colleagues.

(2) Think about the items on your long-range "to do" list and jot down new ideas to try in class. (The ideas for some of my best in-class activities have come during meetings.)

(3) Write down notes for an article, short story, or letter to the editor you'd like to write.

(4) Brainstorm possibilities for reaching a student who's not doing well in one of your classes.

(5) Plan exam questions for one of your courses.

(6) Figure out ways faculty meetings could become more effective and productive. Share your ideas with the principal. In the routine hustle and hassle he/she may not think of doing things another way but would be willing to try something someone else suggested.

(7) Work on a report that's due soon.

(8) Revise and update your "to do" list.

You get the idea, I'm sure. You may not be able to get up and leave the meeting, but you can use the time you're trapped there for productive thinking. What's more, you won't be so frustrated and angry about meetings that go on too long once you see that the ideas you hatch at those times really do pay off.

BENEFITTING FROM DUTY TIME

Most teachers see duties as just another way their time is wasted on the job, but unless your school district has the money to hire monitors and aides, duty time is a fact of life.

Study halls aren't too bad if the students are reasonably well behaved. (See Chapter Four for tips on classroom management.) You can correct papers, read, and hold conferences with individual students. But many teachers are stuck with bus, hall, or cafeteria duty where they have to walk around, anticipating and preventing problems, and confront students who are in the wrong. There's little hope of getting papers graded or reports written if you're assigned to a duty where you have to be on your feet and on the prowl.

What you can do, however, is use the time to get to know your students better and, by doing so, improve your ability to work with them in the classroom. Forget about playing policeperson and assume the role of friendly adult supervisor. Chat with the students who tell you (and whose grades and homework record confirm) that they hate math, history, or English. Find out what they do outside of school or what they plan to do when they finish school. There's too little time for conversations like these in the classroom and they can be very worthwhile. Besides gathering information that you can use to make your subject more relevant, you're showing students that you care about them as people. Often, they'll respond by working harder in your class, and you'll spend less time dealing with behavior problems, sending warning notices, and arranging makeup tests for chronic absentees.

Even if you don't have the opportunity on duty to chat with students you have in class, you can gain a great deal of insight into students' social relationships just by watching them interact with each other in an informal setting. Anything you observe about their dress, their language, their social groupings, and their interaction with other adults, such as cafeteria workers and administrators, will give you clues about them which you can use to good advantage in the classroom. If you're an English teacher, for example, you can draw on such observations to help students select topics for personal experience essays. Or you may finally find a way to compliment a student who's always been in your classroom doghouse when you see him stop to help a younger student who just dropped his lunch tray.

Hall and cafeteria duty time is also useful for reinforcing and reminding students about class work and behavior. When Johnny walks by, say hi and thank him for his contributions to the class discussion today. Smile and tell Janie you're looking forward to reading the report she said she'd turn in tomorrow. (Don't mention anything about the fact that it's two weeks late. Your purpose here is only to remind.)

You'll have to put the duty time in anyway, so it makes sense to have it count for something. If you look for ways to tie things in, you'll find them. Duties offer teachers the opportunity to extend and improve their relationships with students. Take advantage of this opportunity even though you didn't choose it and see how it can make life better for you and your students in the classroom.

HINTS FOR HOMEROOM

Administrators see homeroom as an efficient way of collecting and communicating necessary information. Teachers, on the other hand, view homeroom as a necessary evil. You can save yourself time and hassle and win the hearts of your administrators at the same time if you set up a routine to deal with the homeroom tasks quickly and accurately.

Homeroom duties usually fall into four categories: (1) attendance, (2) announcements, (3) collecting information from students, and (4) conveying information to them.

If the daily announcements are printed rather than read over the P.A. system, appoint a student to read them and free yourself for other tasks. Rotate the job periodically and always have an alternate available in case of absence. Make it clear to the students on the first day that you expect everyone to sit quietly while the announcements are read. You can't force anyone to listen, but you don't want someone in the room to miss an important notice just because several other students had little or no interest in the subject. (Yes, we should teach manners. Some students don't have the opportunity to learn them anywhere else.)

The key to dealing with the other tasks is seating students in alphabetical order. If students balk at this requirement, explain that you don't want to cause them grief by marking them absent by mistake or forgetting to give them a needed form. Students will usually accept your explanation. After all, the homeroom period only lasts for five or ten minutes anyway.

Most schools insist that teachers, not students, take attendance. I always thought the rule was silly until one day my class attendance record for a particular student was requested for use in a police investigation.

Apparently, the student was leaving school during the day to break into nearby houses. Although I never had to testify in court, I realized then that should I have to at some point, I wouldn't be comfortable swearing to the accuracy of the records when I had delegated that responsibility to a student.

Once students are seated alphabetically, you can do almost everything very quickly and painlessly anyway.

(1) Make a seating chart and establish a homeroom folder. Keep it in the vertical file holder on your desk or in the top drawer.

(2) Before students come into the room, pass out any forms, notices, and so forth that have to be distributed on students' desks.

(3) After the bell rings and students are in their seats, take attendance by looking on the seating chart for the names of the students whose desks are empty. (Students can be listening to the announcements while you do this.)

(4) Write the names of absentees on the absence slip and keep it handy in case a student comes in late.

(5) Record the absences by writing the date by the absentees' names on the seating chart. If a student comes in late, mark a "T" beside the date. When a student returns from an absence and shows you the excuse slip issued by the office, circle the date.

(6) As you record each day's absentees on the chart, quickly check to see if you have any which should be circled and aren't. If so, ask the student for a slip, sending him/her to the office if necessary.

(7) Pick up the forms from the empty desks, write the names of the absentees on them, and put them in the homeroom folder to give to students when they return.

(8) When you have forms to collect from students, walk around the room and pick them in alphabetical order. At the same time, jot down the names of students who don't turn them in. Add the names of absentees to this list and clip it to your seating chart until all the names are crossed off.

If you set up this kind of a routine, you'll find that passing out and collecting forms can be done very efficiently. Students who are absent won't be forgotten, and you'll always be able to answer questions from the main office about who was where and who turned what in. When homeroom is over, put the folder back in your vertical file and you'll be all set to go tomorrow. You may be surprised to find you have a couple minutes left to plan for first period even on a day when you have to collect and alphabetize health cards for every student while the teacher across the hall is still trying to collect cards from some of her students as they rush out of the room to first period class.

FROM HOME TO SCHOOL AND BACK

Having things organized at home and at school won't help you much if what you need at school is something you forgot at home or vice versa. Whatever you use to transport things back and forth, attaché case, tote bag, or duffel, get into the habit of carefully checking your desk at school before you leave to make sure you have everything you need. If you think of something during the day that you want to take home, put it in your bag right then. Do the same thing at home. Leave your travel gear in a convenient place so that you can put things there when you think of them. Then at night, not in the morning when you may be running late, check your work area and make sure you have everything you need for school in the bag or attaché case. Put it somewhere near the door so that even if you oversleep and aren't thinking too clearly, you'll stumble over it in the morning. Be especially sure that your calendar, which is absolutely essential, always travels with you.

ADMINISTERING YOUR TRIVIA

Passes, paper, and procedures can drive you crazy. Without advance planning in setting up systems that you stick with long enough for them to become routine, you'll end up frazzled by the end of the day. If you try to respond to the demands of several students at once as you hunt for the pack of hall passes which must be buried in the homework papers you collected last period, you create a chaotic atmosphere which leads to more problems you'll have to spend time dealing with. The key to avoiding all this confusion, of course, is organization.

The first rule: When students come into the room, they go to their seats and begin working. (Suggested activities to use during this time appear in Chapter Four.) If they need to talk to you about anything, they must wait until everyone is quiet and busy before coming up to your desk one at a time. Some teachers have students sign up on the board or a sheet of paper and then go to students at their desks in the order in which they signed up.

The second rule: Put everything from the previous class away before getting out any materials for the next class.

Class Folders

Set up a folder for each class and keep them in the vertical file holder on your desk or in the top desk drawer. I prefer folders with two pockets inside because I can keep seating chart, lesson plans and notes on one side and student papers, tests for students who were absent, and handouts to distribute on the other side. Keep everything for one class in one folder.

If you find you collect too many papers to conveniently stuff into one folder, cut off the end of a large (9 x 12) manila envelope, label the envelope with the course name and period, and use it to hold all the student papers you collect. (And keep it *with* the class folder containing other information for that class.)

Since students in my writing classes frequently hand in several different assignments at once, I devised a method to keep them separated. Using a bold felt-tipped marker, I labeled five large sheets of oak tag at the top: writing log, journals, drafts, final copies, and rewrites/makeup. I spread these sheets out on a table and students put their papers in the appropriate piles. When I pick them up all in one stack to put in my class folder, the writing logs are altogether and separated from the journals by the oak tag sheets. I don't need to waste time later to sort them out before checking them off in my grade book.

Seating Charts

Some teachers don't bother with seating charts, but besides having them available for substitute teachers who'll be lost without them, I find they save me time. Students do choose their own seats, but once they've made their choices they must check with me before moving somewhere else. That's because I take attendance as I do in homeroom by looking at the empty seats. By recording absences and tardies on the seating chart instead of the grade book, I am more likely to notice when a student is becoming lax about attendance and can take action right away, e.g. by speaking to the student who's tardy after class. (It helps to have the specifics about dates and times right in front of me. At the end of the quarter I tally the absences and tardies and record the totals in my grade book.) I also note when I issue a bathroom or locker pass to students.

Again, one glance at the chart and I can refuse a request by pointing out to the student that he had to go to his locker one day this week already. When students realize that you won't forget how many "emergencies" they've had, it's amazing how quickly they don't have any. Fewer unnecessary requests from students means less wasted time.

Tips on Hall Passes

Find a secure place to store hall passes and always keep them there. If you don't want to bother issuing so many written passes, get a wooden pass with your name and room number on it. If you have only one such pass, you can easily enforce a policy of just one student out of the room at one time.

Study hall students are even more insistent than students in a class about needing passes to go elsewhere. Establish a similar rule at the beginning of a study period: you will not issue nor talk to any student about a pass until everyone is quiet and working and you have taken attendance. Let students sign up on the board or a sheet of paper when they come in and deal with their requests one at a time.

Even though you are tempted to send potential troublemakers in your study hall to the library just to get rid of them, don't do it. There will be days when the library is closed or they've been banned for disruptive behavior and then you will have to deal with them with no leverage. Use library passes as a way of getting students to cooperate with you. If you want to get work done during this period, students will have to be trained to follow your rules. Announce that you'll give library passes only to those students who come in and get to work quickly and quietly without any reminders from you. Don't make exceptions. Tell the student who dumped his friend's books on the floor while you were taking attendance that, no, he won't be able to go today, but you'll put him at the top of the list tomorrow if he earns the right by using his time wisely today *and* remembers to sit down and get to work tomorrow.

Make Your Own Forms

Although your school probably supplies you with hall passes, warning notices, and other forms, consider making others to save you time on other routine tasks.

By periodically distributing a "missing assignments" form (a sample appears in Chapter Four) as a reminder to students who get behind, you'll have fewer students who fail to complete their work, and parents won't be surprised by low grades on report cards if you also require that they show the missing assignment form to their parents and get their signatures on it. The "afternoon appointment" form is a positive alternative which works better than the more typical detention slip in solving problems with uncooperative students. (See Chapter Four for tips on how to make it work for you.)

A NOTE from

Anne Wescott Dodd

Date: ______________________

To: ________________________

Figure 2. A personalized memo form.

PEOPLE MAKE A DIFFERENCE

Remember that you're not the only one who's burdened by red tape and bureaucratic trivia on the job and that what seems unimportant to you may be very important to someone else. Make friends with everyone on the support staff from custodians and secretaries to cafeteria workers and guidance counselors. Try to help them out when they make requests of you even though you think what they're asking for is a ridiculous waste of time. You'll be amazed at the number of ways these people can save you time and hassles. But grumble, growl, and ignore some task and no one will care if you're in a jam. Smile, say thank you, and take care of the little things on time, and the secretary and custodian will go out of their way to assist you when they can. A cliché to be sure, but you get what you give.

CHAPTER TWO

ORGANIZING YOUR CLASSROOM

The bell rings. Several students crowd around Mr. Booth, all talking at once. "Did you find my notebook in here period two?" "What do you want me to do with this makeup work?" Mr. Booth has a lot planned for class today and would like to get started, but several students still hover around the desk waiting for him to deal with their problems. "I lost my pen, so I can't take the quiz today!" "Mr. Booth, I can't find the lined paper. What am I going to write on?"

WALK DOWN the halls in your school. As you peer into the classrooms, imagine that you're a student. How many look interesting and inviting to you? If you teach in a typical secondary school, what you probably noticed was the sameness of the rooms: teacher's desk front and center, student desks lined up in rows, bulletin boards covered unimaginatively with magazine photos and notices, drab walls enlivened occasionally by commercially made posters, bookcases filled with aging textbooks, and windowsills and shelves serving as storage space for disorganized piles of "stuff."

Dull, impersonal classrooms won't motivate students to learn, and, although creating a comfortable, attractive, and functional classroom won't by itself guarantee that either, you can increase the possibility by making some changes in your room. Don't underestimate the importance of the first impressions students, administrators, or visitors get when they walk into your classroom. Consider what you'd like your classroom to say about you and how you can make it a more pleasant and convenient place for you to work.

CLEAN UP AND FIX UP

Begin with the basics: clearing out, cleaning up, and painting. During the summer the custodial staff usually takes care of general cleaning and polishing the floors. But the maintenance crew may have done nothing about your battle-scarred walls and bulletin boards, and no custodian would dream of touching any of the books and teaching materials. So, first things first. Get rid of everything you don't need: last year's student projects, old textbooks, and the like. Throw away what you can and donate unused books to another teacher or enlist the custodian's help to find another storage space for them. A warning: don't discard any textbooks without getting permission from someone higher up to do so. Most school districts have very specific procedures for disposing of surplus property which includes textbooks, and some teachers have found themselves in the middle of big controversies when citizens have discovered books stamped with a school's name at the local dump!

Paint the Walls

Where there's a will, there's a way even when the principal says there's no money available to have your room painted. One principal who told me that at first later scrounged up a few dollars for paint and gave his okay for me and some student volunteers to do the job ourselves. I felt the few hours after school were a good investment. Not only did I have soft blue walls to look at every day instead of institutional green, I also found that by getting to know the students who helped me paint, I was better able to motivate them in class. If your principal can't find a way to supply the paint, look to a parent or community member for a donation, or ask students for ideas on how together you might find money elsewhere for the project.

Add Some Plants

Get some plants for those cleared-off windowsills. A little greenery especially in the middle of the winter will do wonders for everyone's spirits. Inviting students to contribute plants and asking them to take care of them is a good move. You won't have any extra work, and if some students have a personal investment in the classroom, they'll work to keep other students from tossing litter on the floor and marking up walls and desks.

ARRANGING FURNITURE AND USING SPACE

What you do with classroom space can make a positive difference in students' attitudes, reduce the number of problems you confront, and provide ways for you and the students to use time more productively.

Student Desks

Imagine being the student who spends several hours a day in rooms where the desks are lined in rows. You sit somewhere in the middle of the room. You can see the teacher talking, sketching diagrams and scratching notes on the chalkboard, pointing to foreign countries on the map, but never do you get a full view of what's going on. You're always looking past the heads and shoulders of the students who sit in front of you. Perhaps the teacher tells the class she's disappointed that students won't get more involved in class discussions. You don't like them much because your classmates in the front speak so softly only the teacher can hear what they say. Sometimes you can't even tell who's talking since you can never see anyone's face. To catch a glimpse of students seated behind you, you have to twist around in your chair. The teacher's the only one who can see everyone and really knows what's going on. Thus, what the teacher calls a class discussion is usually nothing more than a series of dialogues.

Consider how your class discussions might be improved just by arranging the desks so that students can see each other as well as you. There may not be enough room for a circle in your room, but even a double-tiered semi-circle or horseshoe arrangement is more conducive to class discussions than rows. If students do a lot of small group activities, setting up several smaller circles or making "tables" by pushing a few student desks together will save time.

The Teacher's Desk

Even if you want to keep the student desks in rows, the front of the room is not the best place for the teacher's desk if you want the best classroom control. Put a small table in the front near the chalkboard to use when you are presenting information to the whole class at once and move your desk to the back or side of the room. That way you'll have an edge on students when they take tests or work individually at their desks. The mischievous students will have to turn around to see if you're looking at them before doing anything they know is not allowed. The curious or the easily distracted students will be less likely to notice when you're talking with one of their classmates at your desk. Since none of them can see you, they won't know at a glance when you're checking on them.

Teacher's "Office"

Unless you're a department head, you probably don't have your own office at school, but you can create one quite easily in your own classroom. If the room design allows it, move your desk to a back side corner close to the doorway to the hall. If not, look for another space where you can put your desk and file cabinet and use a bookcase, windowsill, or table for your reference books and supplies. Take over the end of a nearby bulletin board or wall space for the clips to hold daily bulletins and absence lists and other items, such as a calendar, which you need to refer to. When you put the furniture in place, try to limit the access to the space behind your desk so that you have in fact made a little office, with the front "wall" actually the front of the teacher's desk. Place a chair or student desk at the open side of your desk to use for student conferences. Although the physical layout in your room may pose some obstacles, with a little creative thinking, you should be able to find a way to get everything you routinely use, need access to, or must control, such as supplies, near at hand.

Reading Area or Conversation Corner

Elementary teachers know the value of setting up areas in the room where students can work on specific activities. Although most secondary teachers probably won't want to establish learning centers like those which are common in the early grades, setting aside a corner of the room as a reading or conversation area is beneficial, especially to social studies or English teachers and others whose students work in small groups.

I picked up a 9′-x-12′ rug in fairly good condition that someone had put out for the weekly trash collection and brought it to school. Using it to define the small group area in the rear of the room, I added two comfortable chairs and a loveseat which I got from people who no longer wanted them in their homes. Not only was the area a comfortable place for students to read if they finished their assignments early, it was the preferred place for small groups to work. Because the corner was off limits to individual students who were behind in their work or otherwise failing in their classroom responsibilities, it served to motivate some students to work harder. All students were able to work there on small group projects, but the groups, of course, had to take turns. This area also turned out to be a pleasant place for me to talk with problem students, other teachers, and parents after school. Difficult meetings with students or parents seemed to go better in this relaxed, informal area than they did when we sat in the stiff-backed student desks.

A PLACE FOR EVERYTHING

When you plan your classroom, think about what other things need space as well as ways you can encourage and reward learning by your students.

Lost and Found

Get a box for all those stray books, notebooks, and whatever else students leave behind that you don't know what to do with. To make it more attractive, cover it (or ask a student volunteer to do so) with self-stick adhesive covering and boldly label it "Lost and Found." Set aside a place for it, and tell students that's where you'll put everything they leave behind. That way, no one will have to bother you to ask if you have seen whatever. Students themselves can check the box for the missing item.

Supplies

Supplies present several problems. Getting them at the beginning of the year is not usually too much of a problem, but later in the year some needed items may be in short supply. To avoid not having what you need when you need it, always have a backup. For example, besides the pack of lined paper you are currently using, keep one or more unopened packs on hand and get a new supply as soon as you begin to use the last unopened pack.

Keep the supplies in an area where you have control over them. Put a pile of paper out so that students can help themselves, but keep the rest of the paper in your "office" where students aren't permitted to be without your permission. Let students know where they will find what they need so they don't have to ask you every time they want a sheet of paper. If you get into the habit of checking the open supply at the beginning of the day, you won't be interrupted later. If the open supply is on a table or shelf near your desk, students will be less likely to take more than they need. You can do your part for conservation by making a stack of scrap paper (dittoed pages that come out too light, get wet, or aren't needed anymore) available, too.

Get a small box or cover a can to hold scruffy, short pencils that no one would want to keep for the students who come to class unprepared. The fact that these pencils are undesirable encourages students to remember their own the next time. If you loan pencils in good condition, most of them will disappear. Tell students where they can find these so they won't have to ask you and remind them that they must return what they borrow at the end of the period. Even if some forget, in most cases the supply will maintain itself if you also add the pencils and pens you find left behind in the room.

Makeup Work

Another timesaver is a collection point for makeup work. A box clearly labeled and kept near your desk will help prevent papers from getting lost or mixed in with others on your desk. At the end of each period, however, be sure that you empty the box and put the papers in the folder or envelope for that class. To avoid problems with students saying they turned work in which you've never seen, tell students that important assignments, such as term projects, should never be placed in the box or left on your desk; students must hand them to you personally.

Classroom Library

The classroom library provides an option for students who finish work early, one that doesn't require you to do anything once you've set it up in the first place. Ask students to donate magazines and books related to your subject area or which are of some general educational value, contribute some yourself, and set aside an area in the room (the reading/conversation corner, if you have one) where students may go to find something to read whenever they have free time. If you have items in the library which you don't want to lose and students may want to take home, set up a sign-up system for borrowing magazines and books. A card file can be used for books, while a notebook might serve the purpose for magazines. Appoint a student librarian in each class to supervise checking out/returning of items and to make sure everything's in order at the end of the class.

Classroom Museum

Some subjects, such as science, offer good possibilities for classroom displays. Consider your room a museum as well as a classroom. Invite students to bring in items related to topics you're studying for temporary or permanent display. You may want to place these all around the room or set up a museum corner. However you display the rock collections or birds' nests, encourage students to study and learn from these displays when they finish their work before the rest of the students.

Publishing Student Work and Posting Information

"Publishing" student work, that is, making it available for others to see either in print or on display, is a wonderful way to motivate students to work harder than they might if the teacher is the only one who will see the finished product. Work may be done by individuals or by small groups.

(1) BULLETIN BOARD DISPLAYS: Put students in charge of sections of the bulletin board instead of doing the work yourself. Ask for student volunteers with talent in art when you need decorations, or give individual students or small groups the responsibility of coming up with something interesting for a certain section of the bulletin boards. Rotate the jobs so that every student participates during the year. (This is yet another way of helping students see the classroom as theirs as well as yours.) Producing a bulletin board display can always be an option when you assign unit projects.

(2) GRAFFITI BOARD: When you find the class in between bulletin board displays (e.g. Christmas is over but the next small group hasn't had time to finish getting their display together), put up some blank sheets of newsprint and invite students to contribute poems, quotations, drawings, or whatever they find interesting. (Be sure you set some ground rules beforehand about what constitutes appropriate classroom language and "art.")

(3) SMALL GROUP PUBLICATIONS: Have students work in small groups to produce an issue of a magazine, newsletter, or newspaper for which they select a name. The publication can be done as a science newsletter, a newspaper as it might appear at a particular time in history, or a literary journal. One small group can do all of the work themselves or act as an editorial board and request submissions from everyone in the class. All groups don't have to produce publications at the same time; perhaps a different group can be responsible each quarter. Another variation (and a good public relations technique) is a newsletter for parents containing information about class activities and assignments.

These publications may be printed in multiple copies so that everyone in the class gets one, but a copy should also be posted on the bulletin board for all your classes to see. Make other copies available in the reading corner for them to read. The student authors will delight in the responses they get from a larger audience.

The whole publication may instead be "published" on the bulletin board for people to read in the manner of the Chinese who instead of getting individual copies of the daily newspaper read those which are posted around the city.

Class newsletters should be distributed to the parents, of course, and also to the school library, principal, department head, and guidance office. They can do a great deal for students' self-esteem and your reputation as an interesting and effective teacher.

(4) CLASS NOTEBOOK: When students do a very good job with a written assignment, anything from an answer to an essay question on a test or research paper to an original short story or poem, ask them to give you copies for the "Class Notebook." The notebook is nothing more than a three-ring binder divided into sections, one for each kind of writing collected. Keep the class notebook in the reading corner for students to browse through when they have free time. Not only will you be rewarding the students who do well by inviting them to contribute to the notebook, you'll also build a collection of samples to share with classes next year when you're explaining a new assignment.

(5) TV LISTINGS: Students probably watch too much TV, but you can improve the quality of what they watch and extend their learning in your subject area by checking the TV listings and making a list of quality programs that will be on during the coming week. Post the list in the same place every Monday and invite students who watch programs on the list to earn extra credit by writing or talking about the program they watched. Once you start doing this on a regular basis, you'll probably be surprised at the number of students who check to see what you post and then take the time to watch them. (Now that so many homes have VCRs, perhaps a student can tape an especially appropriate program, such as a production of *Romeo and Juliet,* for the whole class to see.)

(6) STUDENT-MADE POSTERS: Replace the slick commercially produced posters in your room with ones made by students. Make them options when students are choosing projects to do or invite artistic students to create some for extra credit. Students can come up with some really colorful and interesting ways to illustrate quotations, such as "Today is the first day of the rest of your life," lines from poems or novels, their own poems, or warnings against smoking or drug abuse. Because other students respond in a more personal way to work produced by someone they know, they give the student artists/writers some much needed and appreciated recognition.

All of your efforts to make students feel better about themselves by displaying what they do will have payoffs in your classroom. You'll see students try harder on other class assignments, get along better with you and their classmates, and take better care of the classroom, all of which will help to make your job easier and more rewarding.

CHALKBOARD TIPS AND ALTERNATIVES

If you use the chalkboard as an aid when presenting information, consider the following:

(1) Write the information you want students to see on the board before class. That way it will be clear and evenly written, and you won't have to turn your back if the class is a difficult one that needs close supervision. Use a different color of chalk to highlight points as you talk and help keep students focused on the point.

(2) If you don't want students to see the information when they first come into class, erase what you have written but lightly enough so you can still read what you had there even though the students in the front row cannot. During class when you write over the lightly traced letters again, your writing will come out even and legible. Or you might consider doing what my grade school teachers used to do: pull the map or movie screen down until you are ready for students to see what you have written on the board.

(3) Reserve a section of the chalkboard to write down homework assignments and beginning-of-class activities. (Examples of the latter appear in Chapter Four.) Students can depend on finding certain information in specific places.

(4) Even though you think high school students are too old to want to help out by cleaning boards, ask them. You may be surprised at their response. Besides, teachers are too busy to do everything themselves, especially when students can benefit by sharing with such chores.

If you don't like using the chalkboard because you like to prepare things at home, consider using an overhead projector.

There is yet another option for those who are sure they're allergic to chalkdust and extremely uneasy about using anything that has to be plugged in or fiddled with. Get an easel with large sheets of paper or one of the erasable boards made to be used with bold felt-tipped markers.

A CURE FOR MID-YEAR BLAHS

Actually, this "cure" can be used anytime you want the feeling of a new beginning. Don't just change the decorations on your walls and bulletin boards. Change all the furniture around. Make blank seating charts to fit the new arrangement of student desks and when the students come in the room, pretend it's the beginning of the year again. In all classes except homeroom let students sit wherever they like and write their names down on the chart. (Remember, there they have to sit alphabetically unless you want extra work to do.) Even if you had separated Dennis and Diane, let them try again. If it's the start of a new quarter or semester, you can really make yourself and students believe that everyone has a brand new start. Dennis and Diane may be able to make it this time. At the very least the change will perk everyone's spirits up for a time. (If someone else uses your room one period, give that teacher a blank copy of your new seating chart and explain why you've changed everything around.)

IF YOU DON'T HAVE A ROOM TO CALL YOUR OWN

You may be one of the teachers who has the real disadvantage of teaching classes in several rooms. Because the rooms belong to someone else, you'll have to forget about doing most of what has been suggestd here. Here are some ideas though.

(1) Get a rolling cart (like ones AV aides carry the TV and movie projector) and wheel everything from room to room.

(2) Ask the teacher in each room if there's a file or desk drawer you can have. Once I wasn't able to get even that much space, so I put a box (a hanging file box would be especially good) in every room in which I had a class. After school or early in the morning when I had materials, such as dittoed sheets I had just run off, I would travel around to each room and put what I needed for that class in its box. I made sure everything I needed was in those boxes and carried less with me during the day.

(3) You'll have to designate some space as your "headquarters." One of the teachers involved will probably be able to give you a corner where you can put a small desk or table to function as one. If not, even a corner of the teacher's room will do. Again, put a box there where you'll keep everything that doesn't go with any specific class or that you don't need to carry with you. As long as you're a traveling teacher, you'll probably be better off keeping most resource files at home, but you still need a central place to which you have access first thing in the morning, other times throughout the day, and the last thing at night to drop things off

and pick them up. A classroom might not work for this purpose if you can't work there during your prep period or you don't want to interrupt someone else's class to get something you forgot. What you'll have to do to stay organized is reduce the number of things you carry around and establish a routine of going to your "headquarters" to switch the books and folders you're carrying from one class to those for the next one. What for other teachers is simply a matter of clearing off a desk may be a trip around the school for you.

(4) Don't feel that you must keep the student desks in rows for your classes just because it's someone else's room. Train your students to rearrange the desks however you want them as soon as they come in the room and to return them to rows at the end of the period. It really isn't a big deal if students do all the work, it doesn't take more than a minute or two, and, chances are, the teacher who "owns" the room won't even know they've been moved.

(5) Do ask for bulletin board and chalkboard space which your class can call its own. Most teachers will be glad to give up worrying about what to put on the bulletin board, but you may run into problems with the chalkboard, especially if space is limited. In that case, consider using an easel or an overhead instead. (The industrial arts teacher might be willing to have his students make an easel for you and someone in the school can steer you to a paper supply source.) In the unlikely event bulletin board space is at a premium as well, look around the school for a bulletin board in the hall or library that no one's using. Even though you don't have a place to call your own, you can still see that your students' work is displayed.

(6) Don't despair. When you get some seniority, you'll probably get your own classroom. Many of us as beginning teachers went through the trials you're enduring now. And think of it this way: If you can keep it all together as you teach in several rooms, you can do just about anything anywhere!

PLEASANT SURROUNDINGS MAKE A DIFFERENCE

Both you and your students need an attractive, comfortable, and convenient place to work. Schools are often compared to prisons, and some classrooms actually look as uninviting as oversized prison cells. Research has shown that people respond—positively or negatively—to their surroundings, and that even the color of the walls can make a difference. (Pink, for example, works to calm anxious, restless individuals.) While you may not be able to measure the effect of your efforts to improve the way your classroom looks, you'll feel better about your work if you personalize the place where you spend a large chunk of your time each day.

CHAPTER THREE

PLANNING AHEAD TO GIVE YOURSELF A BREAK

As Suzanne grabs a quick cup of coffee before the bell, her friend says, "C'mon, Suzanne. You can take ONE night off. This is the last night the movie's on. You missed a great one last week, and it'll be quite a while before you can see them on your VCR."

"I can't. I've got too much to do — three sets of tests to grade, handouts I need typed by tomorrow, and that curriculum survey to fill out before the department meeting. Next time, I promise."

"Next time it will be something else."

IF YOU TAKE the time in advance to carefully and creatively develop lesson plans for your classes, you will save time and aggravation later. People who aren't used to doing things ahead often don't realize this simple fact. Ironically, their failure to plan leads to a "Catch-22" situation: they're so swamped with routine tasks and unanticipated problems, often caused by the lack of planning in the first place, that they end up so tired and irritated that they can't plan, and so it goes.

By thoughtfully planning all your classes in advance, you can (1) increase student achievement and motivation, (2) improve student behavior, and (3) balance your workload.

Summer and school-year vacations provide the time you need to do this advance planning. You may say, "Vacations to do school work? By the time a vacation rolls around, I need to relax, get away from it all just to regain my sanity. If I spend my whole vacation doing school work, I'll still be in lousy shape when I go back." Maybe not.

First of all, you don't have to give up the whole vacation. Spending only a day or two planning ahead, time you would probably do little more than sleep late, watch TV, read, and perhaps snack too much can make some future school days almost as relaxing and enjoyable as vacation days. And counting the weekend days, you'd still have seven days of vacation left for other activities. If you rough out annual plans before the school year even begins, you can arrange your schedule so that you can spend the whole winter recess in the Bahamas or on the ski slopes, knowing that there will be no papers to grade when you return. What you're really doing by working ahead is giving up a little time now to get a lot later on, something like earning interest on your initial investment.

The next few sections describe a step-by-step process of planning which can make your work life more pleasant and your workload more manageable.

(1) Write down your objectives and what you'd like to cover in each course.

(2) Develop a master calendar planning sheet for the whole year on which you can outline what will happen in each course so that your plans fit the school district calendar and your own personal schedule.

(3) Work out quarterly schedules of lessons and assignments for each course on individual calendar assignment sheets.

(4) Check these quarterly sheets against each other, make adjustments to balance your workload, and then make final copies of these calendar assignments sheets for your students and you.

PLANNING WITH A PURPOSE

Even if you have taught a course before, at the beginning of the new school year ask yourself these questions, first about each course in general and then about each unit within the course. Consult your notes and plans from previous years and the school district curriculum guide to help you determine what you need to teach.

(1) What are my students like? (Consider ability, motivation, maturity, previous learning experiences, and the like.)

(2) What is my purpose? What content do I want my students to learn? What skills, attitudes, concepts, and values do I want them to develop?

(3) What lessons, reading, activities, and assignments will result in their learning this information or skill, or developing these attitudes?

(4) How should these activities be organized? What do I need to do first? How long will each activity/assignment take? What can students do at home? What should they do under my supervision in class?

(5) How will I evaluate their learning and my teaching? (Written tests are not the only means of determining student progress and teacher effectiveness.)

METHODS AND TECHNIQUES TO CONSIDER

Your students will be more interested in learning and less likely to disrupt the class if you use a variety of methods and find ways for them to make personal connections with the material they are studying. Since students have different ability levels and learning styles, you will increase your chances of reaching more students by selecting a number of different methods rather than depending too heavily on lecture/ discussion or question/answer.

Read through the list below and brainstorm ways you can adapt, expand, combine, and apply these methods and techniques to the specific content you will teach

LECTURE—If you want students to take notes, teach them how.

DISCUSSION—whole class, small group

QUESTION/ANSWER—Include a variety of different types: cognitive memory questions (recall of facts), convergent (thought questions with a single correct answer), divergent (open-ended), and evaluative (dealing with judgment, value, and choice).

If you want students to get more actively involved in class discussions, you need to ask questions which require more than a one-word answer, i.e. divergent and evaluative rather than cognitive memory and convergent questions.

SEMINAR (SOCRATIC DIALOGUE)

ROLE PLAYING/SKITS

SIMULATION GAME—or simulated situation to discuss

CLUSTERING OR WEBBING—This technique is useful for generating ideas for an original piece of writing (see Fig. 3).

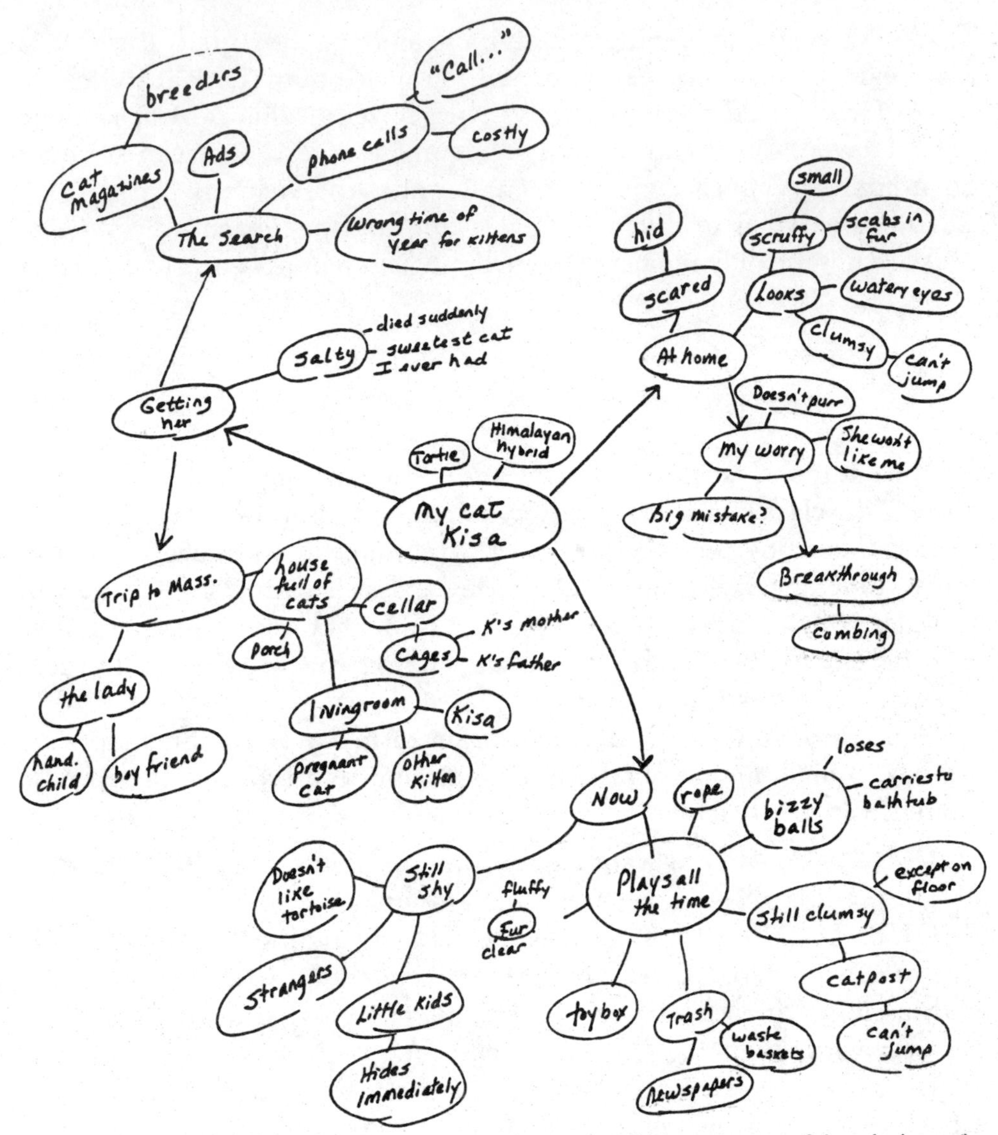

Figure 3. An example of a cluster. Clustering, or webbing, is a useful technique for generating ideas before writing. The subject of this cluster is "My cat Kisa."

CONCEPT OR SEMANTIC MAPPING—Some students prefer this method of outlining because they can visually organize the main points covered in a chapter in the textbook or a lecture (see Fig. 4).

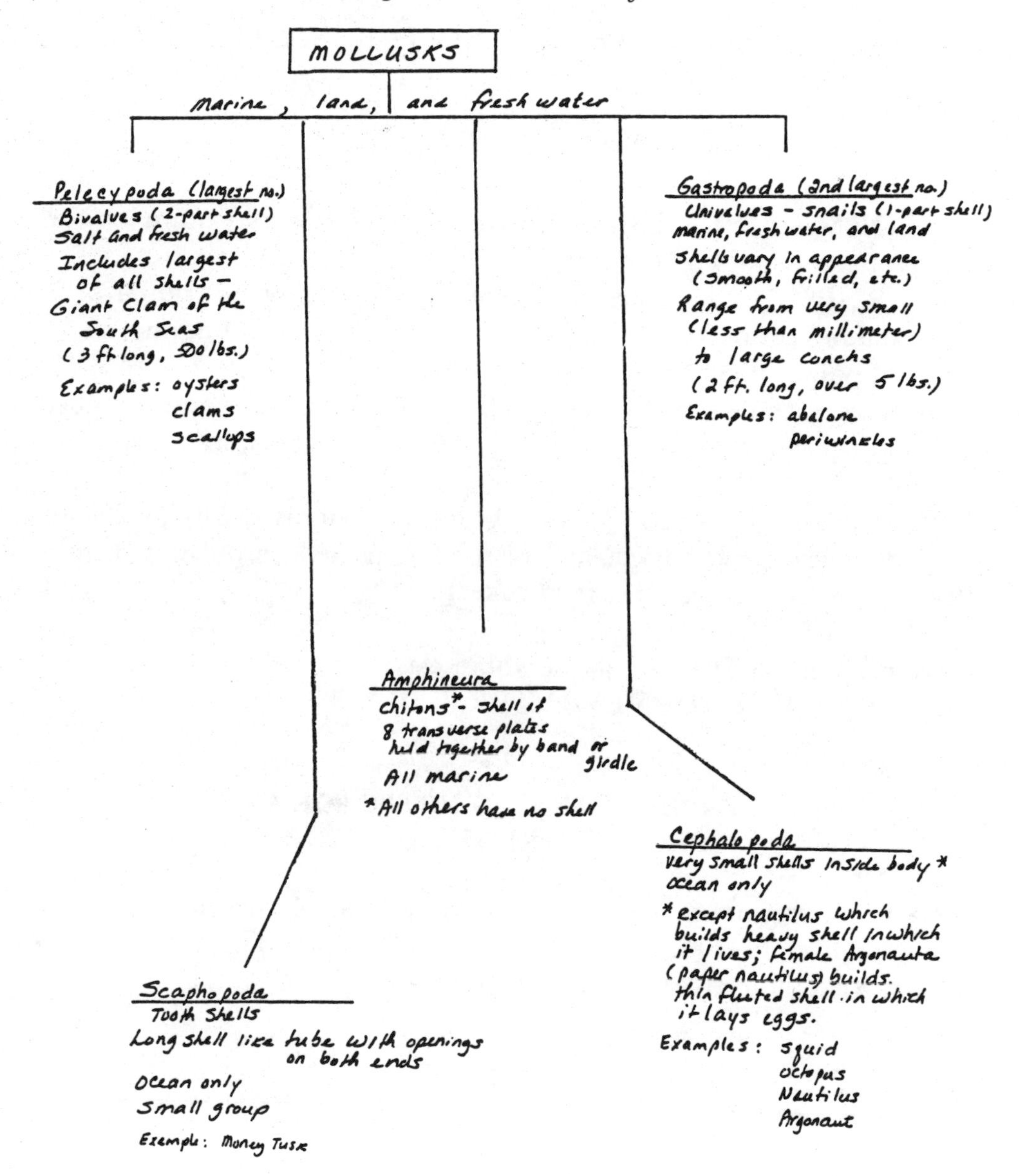

Figure 4. An example of a concept map. The concept map can be used by students to organize and remember information read in the textbook or presented in a lecture.

BRAINSTORMING
PROBLEM SOLVING— individual, small group
PANEL
DEBATE
SPEECH/ORAL REPORT
PROJECT—small group, individual

A-V PRESENTATION—overhead transparencies, film, videotape, filmstrip, slides, recording

DRILL—oral, on paper, on computer

INFORMATIONAL WRITING—essay, review, report, research paper

INFORMAL WRITING—free-writing response or summary for reading assignment, class activity, film viewed, etc.

LEARNING LOG—personal record summarizing individual progress, making connections to what is already known, and noting questions and points of confusion.

CREATIVE OR PERSONAL WRITING—character sketch, short story, play, poem, diary (of a fictional or historic figure), interview, letter, article

PUBLICATION—class-, small group-, or individually-produced newsletter, newspaper, magazine, printed or posted on bulletin board; displays of projects, artwork, field collections

FIELD TRIP

GUEST SPEAKER—or guest whom class interviews

COMMUNITY SURVEY/INTERVIEW

SAMPLE PLANNING NOTES FOR A CREATIVE WRITING COURSE

Here are planning notes for teaching a creative writing course. If your school requires that you use a mastery learning approach, you'll have to write objectives which are much more specific than the ones shown here.

Objectives for Creative Writing

Get students:

- To enjoy writing and realize that they have something to say
- To see that writing is a process, and producing good writing may require several drafts
- To develop fluency in writing without worrying about mechanics except on final copies
- To understand and use figurative language and imagery in their writing
- To understand the structure and form for a short story (plot, character, theme, etc.)

- To recognize the differences between prose and poetry
- To see poetry doesn't have to rhyme by introducing them to a variety of poems and having them write poems of more than one type
- To improve their understanding of writing conventions and their skills in revising, editing, and proofreading
- To talk about and share what they're learning and help each other by working with other students in small groups
- To get personal satisfaction from and recognition for their writing.

Activities

- Write 3-5 journal entries (10-minute free writings per week)
- Form writing groups and work collaboratively on their writing and other tasks
- Read and discuss stories done by previous students and professional writers
- Write an original story (shorter pieces first though: case history, character sketch, dialogue, description, one-sentence plot summaries, one-sentence theme statements)
- Learn from an editing activity and mini-lessons on punctuation, etc., as needed
- Read some poems in a variety of forms; try some of their own
- Talk about poetic devices and do creative thinking exercises
- Write a journal poem (Students keep a journal recording their thinking as they work through several drafts of the poem to final version.)
- Listen to tape of John Ciardi talking about poetry
- Do a mobile or poster poem
- Publish some work by producing a class magazine (all students)
- Publish poster poem on bulletin board and wall; hang mobile poems (all students)
- Contribute some pieces to class notebook (some students)

Evaluation (of student learning and my teaching)

I can determine to what degree my objectives were met by looking at the following:

- questionnaire or survey on their interests/attitudes at the beginning of the course and another at the end
- journal entries throughout quarter which will reveal how they are getting along in the class

- final copies of the pieces I graded
- the work published in the class magazine and elsewhere
- their involvement in the writing process and their behavior during class work sessions
- free writing or questionnaire at the end of the course on what they learned, what activities they liked/disliked, suggestions for me to help plan unit better next time

Time Frame: Nine weeks (one grading period)

Asking for feedback from students at the end of the unit will give you valuable information to use in planning the unit more effectively for another class later this year or next. If your class is not regularly writing journals in which they often reveal how they feel things are going during the course, ask them to do an occasional free writing on the course in general or on a specific activity or assignment so that you can pinpoint problem areas and make adjustments in plans right away.

In order to make the plans for several classes fit together comfortably so that your workload is balanced and your classes are varied enough each day to keep you interested and enthusiastic, do this same kind of general planning for all of the courses and units you will teach.

What's important at this point is figuring out (1) how much time is needed for each unit or topic and (2) what major projects will be included. The next section shows how to use your master calendar to put everything together. (The calendar assignment sheet later in this chapter shows the final creative writing course schedule that was developed from the notes you read here.)

MAKING A MASTER CALENDAR PLANNING SHEET

August is the ideal time to begin, and your master calendar is the starting point. Your calendar, however, will only be as useful as the information it contains. The more you can anticipate now, the more effective your planning will be.

Make up a master calendar planning sheet which shows the school year in weeks. Divide a blank sheet into ten squares, one for each month (see Fig. 5). Using the school district calendar and your own personal calendar, fill in the square for each month on this sheet with any dates which will affect your own lesson plans, such as the beginning and ending dates of grading periods, exam dates, and your own personal plans (a trip out of state during February vacation or the two days in November you'll be away from school at a conference).

September
9/3 Inservice day
9/7 First day for students
9/25 Inservice day

October
10/12 Columbus Day
10/13 Inservice day
10/26 - 10/30 Homecoming activities

November
11/13 Qtr. 1 ends
11/16 Qtr. 2 begins
11/11 Veterans day
11/19 Half-day (parent conferences)
11/26 - 11/27 Thanksgiving recess

December
12/23 - 1/1 Christmas vacation

January
1/29 Sem. 1 ends
1/19 Martin Luther King day

February
2/1 Qtr. 3 begins
2/4 Half-day (parent conferences)
2/13 - 2/21 Winter vacation
2/24 - 2/26 Winter Carnival

March
3/9 - 3/11 Drama Festival
3/18 Inservice day

April
4/15 Qtr. 3 ends
4/25 Qtr. 4 begins
4/16 - 4/24 Spring vacation
4/28 half-day (parent conferences)

May
5/30 Memorial day

June
6/20 Last day for seniors
6/23 Last day of school
6/24 Teacher workday

Figure 5. Master calendar planning sheet. Add other dates (personal and professional) which will affect your lesson planning.

Make sure that you have included everything from the school district calendar (in-services and vacation days, grading periods, exams, and so on), then add all your other personal and professional commitments, such as dates and times for faculty and club meetings, athletic contests and special events, conferences, and so forth. Don't forget about personal activities—weekly tennis dates with a friend, the season tickets you purchased for the local symphony or stage company, the family trip to Disneyworld in February, and the weekend your college friend is coming to visit. If you know that the school's winter carnival occurs in March but you aren't sure of the exact dates, make a general note on the calendar and remember to add the specific dates as soon as you find out what they are. If you kept a calendar during the previous school year, use it to refresh your memory.

This sheet will be your guide in doing your detailed planning for all the classes you teach. Use it to block out times for each unit or topic in all your courses. By noting that information on this sheet, you'll be able to see an overview of your whole year—what each class will be studying when. In case you change your mind about these tentative plans and would like a neat copy for reference when you have done the detailed plans for all your courses, make an extra copy of the original.

On your working sheet, pencil-in some general plans for all your courses before you get down to setting specific dates for tests and projects. Your estimates of time don't have to be exact, but as you jot things down, keep in mind the dates and tasks that are already set. For example, you may want to wait until after Thanksgiving or the beginning of the next grading period to start a new unit. If you end up with a couple days at the end of the quarter, don't worry. That gives you some flexibility to accommodate unexpected events which take away class time. If you don't need those days to finish a unit, you can plug in a useful one- or two-day activity related to the course of change the pace.

Put this master calendar planning sheet aside for now and work on specific plans for each course.

DEVELOPING CALENDAR ASSIGNMENT SHEETS FOR INDIVIDUAL COURSES

To make blank calendar assignment sheets, rule out enough squares to write in the dates (one school day per square) for each of the four quarters in the school year. You'll be making four different calendars, one for each quarter. Using information from the master calendar planning sheet, write in holidays and other dates on which your classes will not meet. Make several copies of these sheets and save one copy on which you don't write anything else so you can make more blanks if you need them. You'll be using at least one sheet per quarter per course for tentatively planning each course and another for a neat master copy of the final plan from which you can duplicate copies for your students (see Fig. 6).

Assignments Creative Writing Quarter Four

Monday	Tuesday	Wednesday	Thursday	Friday
April 11 Begin F.W. and H.W. Grade H.W. Read pp. 1-35 <u>The Craft of Fiction</u>	12 Plot summary exercises H.W. Write a case history.	13 Arena Scheduling– No class	14 Arena Scheduling - No class	15 Arena Scheduling– No class * Spring vacation
F.W. Check (3) 25 Char. Sketch Cards H.W. Read pp. 37-45. Write char. sketch from case history.	26 H.W. Read pp. 47-64 and make final copy of character sketch.	27 * F.C. of character sketch due for grade. H.W. Write a dialogue	28 H.W. Revise dialogue and write final copy for grade.	29 * F.C. of dialogue due for grade. H.W. Read pp. 65-72.
May 2 F.W. Check (5) H.W. Write ¶ combining setting and action.	3 H.W. Read pp. 73-97.	4 H.W. Write a scene from two points of view	5 Editing Activity #1 H.W. Read pp. 101-138.	6 H.W. Write story idea. State conflict.
F.W. Check (5) 9 H.W. Write case history for main character.	10 (Writing groups to discuss stories until 5/20) H.W. Plot outline	11 H.W. Begin writing rough draft.	12 H.W. Work on story draft.	13 H.W. Complete draft for Monday.
F.W. Check (5) 16 Checklist for story H.W. Review rough draft and revise.	17 H.W. Work on story.	18 H.W. Work on story.	19 H.W. Finish story. Final copy due tomorrow.	20 * Final copy of story due at the end of the period.
F.W. Check (5) 23 Answerless Questions H.W. 5 concrete and 2 found poems	24 Brainstorming Clustering H.W. Poem appealing to visual.	25 Sound Devices H.W. Poem using Sound devices	26 Abstraction Exercise H.W. Abstract idea Poem	27 Eve Merriam ditto H.W. Begin journal poem.
30 Memorial Day	F.W. Check (4) 31 Sense devices H.W. Haiku or tanka with sense device underlined and labeled.	June 1 H.W. Journal poem.	2 Ciardi Tape H.W. Journal poem.	3 Ciardi Tape H.W. Journal poem.
Final F.W. Check 6 A = 32 B = 23 C = 9 Ciardi Tape H.W. Journal poem (Seniors) due tomorrow.	Editing Activity #2 7 * Journal poem due (Seniors only) H.W. Journal poem Seniors: Magazine Submission	8 * Magazine submission due (Seniors) H.W. Finish journal poem	9 * Journal poem and other poems due for grade H.W. Mobile or poster poem (due Tuesday)	10 H.W. Magazine Submission.
* Magazine 13 Submissions due H.W. Finish mobile or poster poem.	14 * Poster poem (or mobile) due Work on class magazine.	15 Work on class magazine	16 Work on class magazine	17 Finish class magazine.

Figure 6. An example of a calendar assignment sheet distributed to students.

Beginning with the course where you have the least flexibility to move things around, consider one course at a time. Using the planning notes you made earlier and fill in the assignments and activities for that course on a blank calendar assignment sheet for the first quarter. (You may not want to do the whole year's plans before school starts. Save the forms for the other quarters to do later. It will save time for you, however, to fill in the dates now so that the sheets will be ready when you want to work on the next quarter's plans.)

Use the main part of each square to indicate what will happen in class each day and the bottom of the square to show what students are to work on outside of class. What you'll have when you finish is an outline of the whole quarter which will serve as your guide in writing the detailed daily lesson plans you need for teaching and as an assignment sheet for students during the quarter. Don't use ink the first time around though because the plans aren't final yet.

BALANCING YOUR WORKLOAD

Spread out the first-quarter calendars for all your classes along with the master claendar planning sheet which shows school and district events as well as your personal out-of-school activities. You want to be able to see them all at once.

Check what you have scheduled for each day and week. See how one class meshes with the others. What you want to do is stagger your workload so that you have a manageable amount of grading and correcting to do at one time. As you go along, jot down on the master calendar all the major sets of papers you will have to correct and the dates they are due. Besides the papers you will have to correct, also consider what you've scheduled for yourself during the day. Showing a film or giving students a free reading day will require less energy and preparation than delivering a lecture, so it's not a good idea to schedule lectures in all of your classes on the same day.

If you see a day where you've scheduled papers to grade from several classes, change your assignments around so that one class will hand papers in on another day. Also notice when major projects or papers that will require a lot of time to grade will come due and juggle your rough plans so that these will be turned in when you can more easily handle them. You really don't want a set of term projects facing you on the Sunday night you get home from a relaxing but tiring weekend skiing or visiting friends.

This planning and scheduling process is really like putting a puzzle together. You have to keep moving the pieces around, making adjustments here and there, until they all fit. If you've taught the course before, you should be able to do this part of the planning fairly easily. If it's your first time, you're at a bit of a disadvantage, but don't worry, no plans are carved in granite. Besides, teaching is a learning process. When you find out what doesn't work well the first time, you figure out ways to make it more effective the next.

By manipulating the pieces and engaging in a bit of creative thinking, you can make things better for you, and your students, too. If you're not overtired and resentful from too much paper grading all at once, you'll be much more effective in the classroom. Although sometimes students will have to do one assignment before they can understand how to do another, every course plan will contain some assignments which can be changed. You can always extend the scope of a particular lesson so that a unit test will come one day later or give students one less day to work on an out-of-class project. Other ways to achieve a more manageable workload are listed below.

Some Ways to Balance Your Workload

(1) Flip-flop units between classes. Unless you have to teach units or topics in a certain order, have one class study drug abuse while another investigates pollution, and then reverse them.

(2) Stagger routine activities among classes. If every week you plan a current events or free reading day for all classes, assign a different day of the week to each class.

(3) Have small groups within one class do the same assignments at different times. If you want all your students to do book reports once during the quarter, set up a rotating schedule so that only five or six students present an oral report or turn in a written one once a week.

(4) Instead of collecting written projects from every student one quarter and spending several days of the next listening to oral ones, assign half of the class an oral report and the other half a written one this quarter and reverse the order next time.

(5) Stagger due dates for tests and essays. If you give weekly tests or essays to every class, assign a different day of the week to each class. Why carry home five sets of papers to correct when you could probably find time each day to grade one set at school and go home empty-handed?

(6) Schedule major projects in the middle rather than near the end of a grading period. You won't have the burden of correcting them at the same time you have to average grades, and the earlier due date allows time for students who were absent to get them done, freeing you from dealing with incomplete grades.

(7) Avoid having papers due at times when you'll be busy with other activities or away from school. If you're the advisor to the senior play, oral reports make more sense the week you're worried about opening night.

USING THE CALENDAR ASSIGNMENT SHEET WITH STUDENTS

Give copies of the final calendar assignment sheets to students. Show them how they can use the calendar to plan ahead and make more efficient use of their own time. If you know they'll be away for the weekend right before a major project is due, point out that they can get the work done early and avoid being penalized for handing the project in late. If you require that students keep the calendar in their notebooks, they'll have no excuse for not knowing when something is due.

If for any reason, such a last-minute assembly or a day when school is cancelled due to a storm, your classes do not meet or you find that students need to spend more time on a topic than you had thought they would, revise the calendar and let the students know what the changes are. Post copies of calendars for all the classes that you teach and keep them current. You may be surprised to find out that most of the time the calendar will work just as you originally planned.

You can give students everything they need if you put the quarterly calendar assignment sheet together with an information packet for each unit, stapled sheets giving specific directions for completing assignments and other information you would normally give to students as handouts when you teach the unit. Not only will making these packets up save you time since you won't be handing out single sheets several times during the quarter, but students are also less likely to lose a stapled packet, especially if it's already punched to fit their notebooks.

Make up extra copies of the calendar and packet so that you will have them available for new students and parents who are concerned about their children's low grades and want to supervise their work at home. When parents have all the information about due dates and requirements, they can see that assignments get done, saving time and effort. And when you get a note from the office to send down makeup work for a student who's absent, you won't have to spend time writing a long note as other teachers do. Just circle the relevant dates on the assignment calendar and send it down.

THE COURSE NOTEBOOK: A WAY TO KEEP YOUR MATERIALS ORGANIZED

You'll have more material for teaching a unit than the students will. You've probably collected articles, written notes for lectures, and saved copies of previous tests on the topic being studied. To keep all these resources organized and at your fingertips while you teach, get a three-ring binder for each unit or topic you teach. Decide what categories would be most useful and set up a section in the notebook for each category. A detailed table of contents in the front will make it easy for you to locate any item in the notebook. The notebook works better than a series of folders because papers won't get lost or mixed up. If you keep the notebook on your desk, you'll be able to find that article you need to respond to a student question very quickly.

And a reminder: The Class Notebook in which you collect outstanding examples of student work (described in an earlier chapter) is another valuable resource you'll want to use. When students can't figure out from your explanation exactly what you expect on the research paper, let them read samples in the Class Notebook. One example is worth a thousand words!

THE SECRET FOR STAYING AHEAD

There's really nothing magic about staying ahead of things. Don't leave planning until the last minute and don't put things off. It's easier to *stay* caught up than it is to *get* caught up. Use time when you have it to do what needs to be done for the next quarter, a little bit at a time. Many tasks are overwhelming only if you try to do everything all at once right before it needs to be done. Spending a couple of free hours here and there, a weekend afternoon when you have nothing else to do, or a day or two during a vacation week may be all it takes to get everything organized for all your classes. Remember that you *won't spend any more time* than you do now; you'll just put the time in sooner rather than later. The secret for staying ahead is really quite simple: Get into the habit of working ahead.

CHAPTER FOUR

CREATING A POSITIVE CLIMATE AND REDUCING CLASSROOM CONFLICT

"You already have four hours of detention to make up! One more outburst, young man, and I'll send you to the office!" Mrs. Russell bellows.

"I'll save you the trouble, lady!" John shouts back as he gets up from his seat and heads towards the door. He mutters, "This class sucks!" loudly enough for everyone to hear and slams the door on his way out.

DISCIPLINE may be the number one concern of teachers. Even experienced teachers who have learned to handle routine disruptions effectively and haven't faced chaos in the classroom since their first year of teaching sometimes have nightmares the week before school begins. They envision a room full of noisy students throwing books and shouting out the windows, ignoring their pleas to sit down and be quiet. Their fears are never realized. The first day of school passes without major incident. They get caught up in familiar routines, and their nightmares vanish.

Of course, some teachers do find themselves unable to deal with a class of unruly students, but it usually doesn't happen the first day. September is like New Year's. Students and teachers come on the first day with high hopes for a new beginning. They resolve to overcome their failures and bad habits of the past in order to make their year better than last. Like the resolutions people make for the beginning of a new calendar year, most are not kept, but you can make a positive difference for yourself and your students by taking advantage of this general feeling of hope and renewal that everyone seems to share on the first day of school.

You will be more successful in managing your classroom and motivating students if (1) you carefully organize materials and plan your lessons in advance and (2) you show students that you care about them as people, help them succeed, and deal with all of them firmly, fairly, and consistently. Easier said, of course, than done, but this chapter will suggest several ways that you can make your classroom a comfortable, productive, and friendly place where you and your students can enjoy learning together.

BEFORE THE FIRST CLASS

Make sure that you have everything you'll need for the first day carefully organized and conveniently located. List every task that you have to accomplish before the first class. Get to school early so you have time to double-check materials and take care of the items on your list. If you discover that the office wants you to distribute another form to students, put the forms with the others you have ready to pass out and add that task to the homeroom list. You should have several copies of a blank seating chart which fits the arrangement of the student desks. (If you also give a copy to the teacher who has a class in your room when you have a prep period, you're more likely to find the desks in order when you return for your next class.)

Before the first day you should already have checked to see that you have enough textbooks, textbook cards, and handouts. Always plan for a few more students than you expect so you won't get caught short. During the first class you should schedule time to deal with all the administrivia, introduce the course and explain your expectations, and, most important, involve students in a short but interesting activity. When you've done all you can, relax. Go to the teachers' room and have a cup of coffee, but make sure you leave in time to be in your room before any students arrive.

SETTING THE RIGHT TONE ON THE FIRST DAY

First impressions count more than we sometimes realize. How your classroom looks and what you do and say the very first day will set the tone for the whole year. Students will begin forming their ideas of what you and your class will be like the minute they walk into the room. The fact that you took the time to decorate the bulletin board and bring in plants can make students feel welcome, almost as if they are guests in your home. Even the rowdiest of students would hesitate to do in anyone's living room what may be standard behavior for him in a classroom.

If you have arranged the student desks in a horseshoe and moved your desk to the back corner of the room, you're delivering an unspoken message that you're not a drill sergeant against whom they must rebel but a caring adult who will help them learn. Having all the materials you'll need—from office forms to textbooks—organized and ready to distribute indicates that although administrative details are important and won't be overlooked, you won't waste much class time on such routine matters. And there's some carryover from the manner in which you deal with such things as having students complete and hand in student information cards for the office.

Teachers sometimes convey to their students negative feelings about school policies, procedures, and paperwork without realizing that the relationship of teachers to administrators in some ways parallels that of students to teachers. When students see you display a careless attitude toward a request from the office, they may adopt a careless attitude about your policies and procedures and come to class late or fail to meet assignment due dates. Don't underestimate the wide-ranging effects of the teacher as role model.

Stand by the door and greet students when they come in the room. This simple act sends several messages: (1) you are a warm, friendly human being; (2) this is your classroom and you're in charge; and (3) you're ready to teach. If you're rushing around at the last minute rounding up textbooks or hunting for the student information cards, students will get the impression that your class will be disorganized and they won't learn much. Even if today is the exception and not the rule, the image you present to students on the first day will be very difficult to change.

Begin class on time even if some students are still wandering around looking for rooms. Welcome students who enter late, commenting perhaps that it's hard finding one's way around on the first day. Even if one of the students was not lost but talking to her boyfriend, help her out today by providing her with a legitimate excuse so she can start off on the right foot. The fact that class is already underway tells her that she'd better be on time tomorrow.

Be sure that you appear confident and friendly yet businesslike when you first address the class. If you're a new teacher, you may feel scared and nervous. That's perfectly understandable, but don't let the students know that. Pretend you're an actor or actress protraying the role of a seasoned teacher. After all, you are more experienced than your students, you know more about the subject matter than they do, and you are prepared. Since the first things you have to deal with are quite routine, you can handle them easily. Surprisingly, what begins as feigned confidence will probably soon turn into the real thing.

After asking if everyone is in the right place, check your class roster at the same time you make up a seating chart. Ask students to correct your pronunciation of their names and let you know if they prefer to be called by a nickname. Check off their names on the roster and write them in the appropriate places on your seating chart with reminders, if needed, to help you remember how to pronounce unusual names. The seating chart is very important, since you will use it not only to learn students' names but also to take attendance efficiently after today. By showing concern for their names and by making every effort to learn them as quickly as possible, you let students know that you are interested in them as individuals. Besides, saying "John, please put that book away," is much more effective as a deterrent to undesirable behavior than, "You in the yellow shirt. . . ." Calling role is boring for students, so, to hold their interest and help all of you get to know each other as you call their names, consider asking students to introduce themselves briefly by saying a little about their interests outside of school or their favorite books or TV programs.

Student Information Card

You can save yourself a great deal of time when you want to send messages to students or get in touch with parents when there's a problem if you have students fill out index cards with their name, homeroom, home address, phone number, parents' names (often not the same as the student's), and parents' phone numbers at work. You'll be amazed how useful this information can be later in the year. Because students are so accustomed to filling in forms on the first day of school, they won't question your motives for requesting the information now. If you think you'll want to work with students anytime when they have a study period, also ask them to write out their class schedule on the back of the card and to let you know if it changes. All of this information is available in the office, of course, but if you also keep it on file, you can save many unnecessary trips there later in the year when you may have little time to spare. Instead of having students put this information on index cards, you may wish to make it part of a quesionnaire.

ENGLISH III -- PERSONAL INFORMATION

Name ______________________________ Grade ____ Homeroom ____

Parents' Names __________________________ Home Phone _________

Address ________________________________ Work Phone _________

What periods do you have study hall?

What extracurricular activities do you participate in?

Do you have a parttime job? How many hours a week do you work?
What do you do?

What are your interests and hobbies outside of school?

Where else have you lived or traveled?

What newspapers and magazines do you regularly read?

How often do you read books for pleasure?

What kinds of books do you like?

What is your favorite book?

How do you feel about writing?

What kinds of writing do you do outside of school?

How many hours a day (on average) do you watch TV?

What is your favorite program?

List the subjects you are taking this year according to how you feel about them. Begin with the one you like best and end with the one you like least .

How would you describe yourself as a student?

What are your plans after high school?

On the back of this sheet, tell me more about you, your previous experiences with English, what you'd like to get out of this class, and anything else that would help me get to know you better.

Figure 7. An example of a questionnaire for the first day of school.

Take care of all the routine items on your list, passing out books and forms and collecting them. If any of these need to be alphabetized, recruit a student volunteer to help. (You can check later to make sure the task was done correctly.) To avoid a jumbled pile of cards and forms on your desk, collect items systematically and put them in a specific place you decided on earlier. If you don't have to send anything to the office right now, make separate piles: one for things you'll keep; the other for those you'll pass on to the office secretary or department head. Without sacrificing accuracy for speed, try to get all the administrivia out of the way as soon as you can and move on to matters of more substance.

Introducing the Course and Explaining Your Expectations

Tell your students what they will study this year and why. Make the subject sound interesting, even exciting, to them by projecting your enthusiasm for the course content and giving specific examples of how they can use what they will learn now and in the future. Highlight any special activities you have planned, such as field trips or guest speakers. Remember how important this first impression is. If former students have come back to tell you how your course helped them, share their experiences with your present students. There'll probably be one or two students who came into the class disliking the subject. This happens even in elective courses because of scheduling problems or parental pressure. Even though you probably don't know who the students are at this point, address the issue by announcing that you will make every effort to help students succeed and enjoy the class if they will meet you halfway by doing what's expected of them.

Some students will be less interested in finding out what the course will be about, however, than in figuring out just how much (or how little) work they'll have to do to get a good grade or how much they can get away with in terms of handing in late papers, missing class, and the like. Instead of merely talking about these matters, give students a handout which lists course objectives, outlines the course content (or just that for the first unit), explains your grading/attendance policies, and includes any other information that will be useful to them, such as when you're available to give extra help. Putting everything in writing will help you clarify exactly what you expect from them and make it easier for you to be consistent. The latter is very important because students quickly

REQUIREMENTS FOR EXPOSITORY WRITING -- FOURTH QUARTER

1. Three (3) in-class essays (Revised and rewritten and/or corrected)

2. Four (4) final copies of essays (Types to be specified and explained--usually on Mondays) revised and rewritten and/or corrected after they have been graded

3. One (1) magazine submission near the end of the quarter--will be explained--neatly and carefully done as a final copy

4. Attendance at all of the work group sessions or make up absences after school at special sessions to be arranged and most other class periods (More than four excused absences or one unexcused absence will mean a loss of credit on final grade.)

5. Submission of one of your essays on ditto for discussion by the work group. Make sure the ditto reaches me by homeroom period on the date the essay is scheduled for discussion. (You may type your essay and use a pseudonym if you wish.) All other students must have completed rough drafts for each work group session.

6. Wise and consistent use of class time which is to be spent only on writing and related activities. You should be willing to help others and to seek help from them or me. Particular emphasis of this point will be made in reference to work group sessions.

7. Voluntary work, such as exercises to correct problems indicated on your individual diagnosis sheet which you will fill out at the beginning of the quarter.

8. Voluntary free writing--no more than five per week. These will be accepted only at the beginning of the class on Tuesdays through June 12 (last day). They will count as extra credit.

9. Evidence that you have conscientiously been working on your writing and trying to improve it throughout the quarter.

10. Completion of a grade sheet which lists all graded assignments as well as additional ungraded work you have done throughout the quarter.

11. All work must be kept in a folder which contains nothing but materials and writing for this course. Folders will be checked and evaluated during the quarter at unannounced times.

12. Remember that you lose one letter grade for each day a graded assignment is late and that all assignments must be completed for credit in the course.

NOTE : YOUR QUARTER GRADE WILL BE BASED ON ALL POINTS LISTED ABOVE, NOT MERELY THE AVERAGE OF YOUR GRADED ESSAYS.
The second quarter grade will make the difference in your semester grade if the two grades do not average evenly.

Figure 8. Sample of course expectations for an expository writing class.

COURSE EXPECTATIONS -- GENERAL BIOLOGY

General

You are expected to

1. Get to class on time and attend on a regular basis.

2. Make up all work missed due to absence in a timely fashion. (In general, you have one day for each day you were absent. Makeup labs will be scheduled after school.)

3. Complete all assignments in the course and meet scheduled deadlines. (Graded papers lose one letter grade for each day they are late, but you will be credited with a D- if you get the work in by the makeup deadline at the end of the quarter; failure to complete any assignment will result in a failing grade for the quarter.)

4. Participate positively in all class activities.

5. Cooperate with lab partners and do your fair share of the work.

6. Make entries in your learning log at least twice each week.

7. Keep a list of work completed and grades earned throughout the quarter.

8. Keep all of the work fór this course in a notebook.

Grading

Your quarter grade will be based on the following:

Tests and quizzes	50%
Lab Reports	15%
Project	15%
Learning log, notebook, and homework	10%
Class/Lab Participation (includes attendance--You can't participate if you're not in class!)	10%

Note : If you want to know what your quarter grade is before rank cards are issued, you must keep a complete list of your own grades throughout the quarter.

Figure 9. Sample of course expectations for a general biology class.

discover ways to manipulate teachers, and not only does a lack of consistency make it easy for a Machiavellian student to get the upper hand, it can also lead to more serious problems, such as a lack of general classroom control and the fostering of negative attitudes toward you and the course. The handout is very useful for other reasons as well. You don't have to explain over and over again that a student loses a letter grade for turning a paper in a day late. It's all there in black (purple if you used the ditto machine) and white. Post a copy on the bulletin board and require that students keep a copy in their notebooks. When you have a conference with parents whose child is not doing well, give them a copy and they'll be better able to support your efforts at school by helping out at home. Students manipulate parents as well as teachers (and some are very adept at playing one off against the other). That won't be so easy to do when parents understand what you expect.

Further suggestions about what to include in your course requirements and expectations appear later in this chapter and in the next.

Introductory Activity

The first class shouldn't end until students have been involved in a short but specific learning activity. Though there may be days later in the year when nothing much happens in class because the period has been shortened to ten minutes or two-thirds of the students are away on a field trip, you don't want students to get that impression today. You want them to leave with the tacit understanding that in your class they will do something worthwhile every day. You're there to see that they learn something and you won't waste the whole first day on routine tasks or, if you finish early, let them chat until the bell rings.

Possibilities for this activity include everything from giving students an interesting problem to solve or situation to discuss as individuals or as a class, brainstorming a list of ways your subject might be useful to them, filling out a questionnaire (see Fig. 7), or doing a free writing (i.e. writing to get their ideas down on paper without worrying about structure or mechanics) in which they (1) introduce themselves to you, (2) tell you all they know about the subject or the topic of the first unit, or (3) share their previous experiences with the subject, how they did, what they liked/disliked, and what they hope for this year. You can see how these free writings can help you get to know the students better and plan your lessons more effectively. Asking students to share their ideas either orally or in writing is another way you let students know they have value as people. When they sense that you feel this way, they're more likely to respond positively to you and the course and make your job easier by cooperating in class, doing their assignments, and getting to class on time.

BEFORE THE NEXT CLASS

Before the next group of students comes into the room, organize all the materials from this class and put them away or off to the side to deliver to the office. You won't have time now to put things in their permanent locations, so gather up all the papers and index cards you'll be keeping and put them inside the folder for this class. Don't worry about the bulk or lack of organization. As soon as you have a free period or a study hall, you can sift through the bundle, sorting and filing things where they belong. The important point now is to clear your desk of period one *before* you get anything out for period two. Since you don't even know students' names at this point, you will have a hard time later figuring out where stray papers belong. If you've stuffed them all in the appropriate class folder, they'll at least be in the right place.

This point may seem too obvious to mention, but with the fast pace and the vast number of forms and papers to distribute and collect on the first day, it's easy to forget what you're doing. With a simple, but systematic plan, you can keep things organized as you go along and won't have to face an enormous task at the end of the day.

THE FIRST DAY IN STUDY HALL

If you're assigned to supervise a study hall, ask those students to fill out index cards with the same information you requested from students in your class. When you have collected them, hold the pack in your hand and say, "Most of you will have work to do in this period and so will I. We'll need quiet time to get it done. If you don't have any homework, bring a book to read." Explain the procedure for getting passes to leave the room (see "Tips on Hall Passes" in Chapter One), and then say, "I hope that I don't have to use these cards, but if any of you keeps the rest of us from being able to get our work done, I will call your parents. If you don't want me to bother them, then make sure that your actions don't make that necessary."

You may never have to call any parent, but the first time any student disturbs you or other students, *don't* say anything out loud to the whole class. Instead talk with that student privately, at your desk if no one can overhear or out in the hall, and say, in a pleasant but businesslike tone, something like the following: "Susan, your constant talking is making it impossible for me and the other students to get work done. I think you're mature enough to solve this problem on your own, and I'm going to give you a chance to do so. You really don't want me to involve your parents about such a small matter, do you?" Of course, Susan will say no. Continue: "I'm sure you can take care of this matter by yourself. However, I want you to know that if it happens again, I will call your parents."

For most students this conversation will solve the problem. It works better than detention which is a negative approach and punishes you more than the student. If Susan doesn't cooperate, however, *do call her parents the very next time she's talking in class.* (See the suggestions for making such phone calls later in this chapter.) This point is very important, especially at the beginning of the year when you must make it clear to students that you mean what you say. You may be thinking this method is totally unworkable because you can remember a study hall in the past where you would have had to call at least one parent every day. Not true. You may have to make several calls in the beginning and it will take time which you don't want to spare, but the time you take now will gain for you a class period where you can get some work done.

You won't have to call many students' parents because after you've called one, two, or three, the word will get around. Most students of junior high and high school age would do anything to avoid having their parents know that they're creating problems at school. Since most teachers are reluctant to contact parents, they can get away with quite a bit of minor misbehavior without their parents ever knowing. They want to keep things that way, so, if they know you will call their parents if they fool around in your study hall, most will cooperate and save their mischief for another teacher's class or study. Even if you doubt the effectiveness of this discipline strategy, try it and see what results you get. You may be very surprised, and you can almost forget about ever keeping students after school. Later in the chapter you'll see why detention often causes more problems than it solves.

CLASSROOM BEHAVIOR

One of the best ways to motivate students to behave is to treat them as adults. When teachers give to junior or senior high students a list of rules regarding classroom behavior, such as "You are not to talk without raising your hand" or "You must ask permission to get out of your seat," they not only make students feel that they are being treated as little children, they also emphasize the negative rather than the positive.

If You Must Have a List of Rules

If you feel that you must have a list of rules (or if your principal requires that you post one in your room), then on the first day of class ask the students what rules should be established. As the students brainstorm all the rules that would help make the classroom a better place for everyone to learn, you write (or ask a student to do so) them on the chalkboard. No doubt, the students will be much stricter than you would be, but write down everything they come up with.

When no one can think of any other rules to add, ask students to copy them down. Then say, "These are the rules you've established for this class, so I will enforce them. You can consider the list a contract (If the students don't know what a contract is in the "real" world, explain and give an example) you're signing with me. At the bottom of your paper, please write a statement saying that you agree to follow the above listed rules in (name of class). Write the date and sign your name." Check to see that everyone has added this statement, signed, and dated the papers and then collect them. File these in a convenient location. Later when some student fails to follow one of the rules, you can pull out the signed "contract," point to the signature, and say, "Is this your signature?" The student will have to say yes. Rather than give a lecture, you simply remind the student of the particular rule in question and say, "This is a rule the class established and you agreed to follow. What are you going to do about the situation? What do you think I should do?" You can fill in the rest of the conversation. Depending on the situation and student, you may want to give another chance, a warning about what happens next, or a consequence.

A Better Plan

There is a better way, however. When you first meet with students, explain to them that in many ways the classroom is like an office where they all have jobs to do. Ask them what people must do to get along well when they are all working together in the same area. The discussion will probably focus more on displaying good manners than on following specific rules. You can mention, for example, that it's rude to talk or get out of one's seat to sharpen a pencil when someone else is talking to the whole group or disturb the peace and quiet when classmates are trying to work. Also explain that you are responsible for them and can't, therefore, allow them to wander in and out of the room whenever they want to. Tell students that you think they're mature enough to know what's appropriate and what isn't without a list of rules to follow. You simply expect that they will consider other people's needs and feelings in your classroom in the same way they would if they were on the job. You will assume they are responsible and will treat them as mature young adults until they show you that's not the case.

Using this kind of positive approach invites students to cooperate. Most will respond, but, of course, there will be a few students who won't. In order to make sure that they understand what will happen when they make the wrong choices, you should add something like: "If any of you chooses to behave like children, I will be forced to treat you that way. I will discuss the problem with you and give you a chance to correct it, but if that fails, I will be forced to contact your parents. I'm sure you'd rather handle the situation yourself, but I want to make sure you know what to expect if you don't cooperate. Are there any questions about what I expect or what will happen if someone fails to behave responsibly?" Naturally, you will follow through with the announced consequences the first time someone does make the wrong choice.

CLASSROOM ROUTINES TO SAVE TIME AND AVOID PROBLEMS

Rather than deal with recurring matters on a haphazard basis, consider ways that you can set up routines so that students know what's expected and don't have to bother you with unnecessary questions. Explain why they must be sitting in their own seats when the period begins (because you take attendance by looking at the empty seats), how and when they can get paper or borrow a pen or pencil, where to put makeup work they have ready to turn in, what to do when they forget their textbook, when it's appropriate to talk to you about some personal difficulty (*not* when the period is just starting and you're trying to take attendance or pass out paper), and what they should do if they finish an assignment before their classmates do. How you decide to handle these matters will depend partly on your subject area and partly on your personal preference, but you should brainstorm all the matters you can make routine, figure out the best way to handle each, and make these procedures clear to students during the first week or two. (Don't try to cover everything the first day!)

ELIMINATING CONFUSION AT THE BEGINNING OF CLASS

How your class begins has a great effect on what happens later in the period. If students must wait while you take attendance or talk with one of their classmates, some are likely to start fooling around while your attention is elsewhere. You may then have some difficulty getting them to settle down when you are ready to begin the class. The way to avoid such problems is to plan a short activity which doesn't require any explanation from you and which students know they are to begin as soon as they come in the room. You're then free to catch your breath, take attendance, get materials organized, or talk with individual students.

You can set up a schedule of routine activities that matches your general plan for the class or you can tell students to look in a certain place on the chalkboard for the day's activity. (If Tuesday is always individualized reading day, students know on that day they begin reading their books, for example.) Some possibilities:

- a problem to solve (math) or sentence to revise (English)
- a free-writing response to a thought question about the reading they did for homework (can also be used as a reading quiz)
- a logic problem, riddle to solve from a puzzle book, or analogies to figure out from a test prep book (develop thinking skills)
- a free writing on everything they know about a specific topic (good way to begin a new unit)
- a free writing summarizing what they learned in class yesterday
- a concept map on the topic currently being studied (useful way to organize material read in textbook in preparation for class discussion or writing assignment)
- a brainstorming or clustering exercise (helps generate idea for writing)
- a proverb or quotation to interpret or expand
- a list of questions they have about the topic to be studied
- a reading of previous day's class log by secretary (see following text)

DELEGATING TASKS TO STUDENTS

You can cut down on your workload and give students some responsibilities for the class by delegating some of the routine chores to them on a rotating basis. The fact that you trust them gives them a feeling of ownership for the class and helps build their self-confidence. These positive feelings will improve the general atmosphere in the room and motivate students to do the required assignments as well.

Write brief job descriptions for each position and make sure students know what is expected of them. At first you will have to spend some extra time training them to do the jobs, but you'll notice later how much more enjoyable teaching is when small but irritating administrative demands don't sap your energy and enthusiasm before class even begins. Depending upon the needs in your class, you might decide on other titles or positions than those listed below.

Class President/Assistant Teacher: Calls class to order and directs students to work on the beginning-of-class activity; checks homework, notebooks, materials; supervises class if you have to leave the room briefly; assists a substitute teacher.

Secretary: Writes daily log summarizing what was covered in class (like the minutes for a club meeting) and lists names of student who are absent; gets handouts for absentees and makes sure they get them and the assignments when they return; passes out corrected papers.

Room and Supply Monitor: Supervises supplies and general condition of the room by loaning textbooks, pens, and other supplies to students who need them just for the day, passing out blank paper or lab equipment, and making sure the room is in order and litter-free and borrowed materials have been returned at the end of the period.

Librarian: Oversees books and magazines in classroom library; checks them in and out; assists teacher in distributing and collecting textbooks.

HELPING STUDENTS GET ORGANIZED

One of the most frustrating things to hear day after day is "I forgot my homework paper," "I lost my book," or "I left that paper in my math book which is in my locker." Even if you have a supply monitor who can issue pens or textbooks for the period, that won't help if the missing item is a homework paper or if you have no extra copies of the textbook. To reduce the number of such incidents, make bringing all books and materials to class a requirement which counts in the student's grade. Teachers often tell students they want them to do this, but they offer no reward, and penalties occur only when they've heard too many excuses in one day. Students don't like doing anything for nothing and while a good grade is a dubious form of payment, it is payment. This requirement can be made part of a homework grade (see Chapter Five for an explanation). This plan works well with lower ability students, since they can see it's a sure way they can get credit for something they can do even if the subject is very difficult for them. Every little bit of success helps.

Either you or the president/assistant teacher should walk around the room quickly at the beginning of the period to check and see that the students have the following:

- three-ring binder with everything for the class in it
- pen, pencil, and blank paper
- homework paper (if there was a written assignment)

If the president does the checking, he/she can give you the names of those students who are not prepared so that you can record grades in your book: A or F. When students realize that they will actually get or lose credit and that you will check every day, they will bring what is needed. Later in the year you can be somewhat flexible and exempt a student from a penalty for an emergency situation, but if you make exceptions in the beginning, your students will be difficult or impossible to train.

The Three-Ring Binder

Requiring that students have a three-ring binder just for your class is better than allowing for a variety of notebooks and folders. You can punch holes in handouts before you give them to students, and once they're in the notebook, they won't get lost. If students don't have notebooks with folder pockets inside the cover, they should make or buy a folder pocket punched to fit the binder for small papers, such as the type often used in math classes or library and hall passes. Help students divide the notebook into categories (which will vary according to the class and teacher).

What To Keep in the Notebook: calendar assignment sheet in front (perhaps in plastic protector); grade sheet (individual record of grades described in Chapter Five); class notes and handouts; homework; graded papers; and other things, such as journal entries in an English class, lab reports in science, or learning logs (summarizing and reflecting on what has been learned each day or week) in any class. If you have students who lose everything, suggest they also get a plastic pencil/pen case which hooks inside the binder.

Tell students that you will periodically check and grade notebooks at least once each marking period (and don't forget to do so). To get an A for the notebook check, all students have to do is show you that they have everything in the right places and their grade sheets are up-to-date. Even your least able students can handle this requirement, and they are probably the ones who will benefit the most from it.

Of course, you have to spend extra time teaching students organizational skills, but many will not learn on their own. What students learn about organization and responsibility will benefit them after they leave school and save you quite a lot of aggravation now.

WHAT TO DO ABOUT STUDENTS WHO FINISH EARLY

Problems often develop when students have nothing to do. Despite how carefully you plan class activities, some students will finish ahead of the rest. Let students know ahead of time what they are to do when they finish. If you don't want to plan specific assignments or have to explain the next activity to individual students only to repeat the same directions to the rest of the class later, let students know what their general options are, such as reading a book or magazine from the class library, working on a long-term project, doing an extra free-writing response tailored to the topic under study, writing a journal entry, reading from a book they brought to class, or helping you if there are handouts to punch holes in or staple. Make it clear from the beginning that students are expected to be doing something which doesn't disturb anyone else. They won't have to ask you, "What should I do now?" if you tell them ahead of time what their choices are.

MAKING SMALL GROUPS WORK MORE EFFECTIVELY

Perhaps you're one of the many teachers who believe in the value of small group activities because learning to work cooperatively with others is a skill students can use long after they leave school, but after two or three attempts to make them work, you've given up on the idea. Maybe the teacher next door complained about the noise or your students accomplished so little that you felt the time was wasted.

Effective small groups don't just happen. You have to spend time teaching students what their responsibilities are and how to evaluate their efforts. Don't ask them to plunge right into a subject matter task without first letting them practice working together on very short, specific training tasks. Even though these extra activities will take some time away from covering the course content in the beginning, you'll find that students will be able to get more done in their small groups in the end.

Let students know that everyone must contribute to the group and that their individual responsibilities go beyond helping to select one person as chair and another to take notes. Talk about the behaviors that help the group (participating; listening to others; asking questions; staying on task; clarifying, elaborating, or summarizing what has been said; compromising) and those which hinder it (joking or horsing around; monopolizing; criticizing or putting others down; withdrawing by daydreaming, whispering, or talking about unrelated matters). Because even the best students in the class can sabotage a small group, point out that the person who dominates the discussion, allows the group to let him do most of the work, or never says anything obstructs the group's progress as much as someone who fools around or tries to get the group talking about weekend plans.

Practice activities should be challenging but short enough so that you can do several in one class period. After each one, stop to talk about the dynamics of each group so that students will see why some groups were able to finish the task faster than others. Then give them a chance right away to see if they can improve on another task.

Such tasks as calculating the average height in inches or average age in months of group members work very well as the very first tasks because they can be completed very quickly. Other possibilities for follow up include (1) having each student take a turn interviewing another group member (helps students get to know each other), (2) logic puzzles, and (3) coming to a consensus about a topic such as the one improvement most needed in the school or the most realistic (or unrealistic) TV program. (Be sure to explain that *consensus* means reaching a common agreement, not simply deciding by majority vote.)

Have students evaluate how well their group worked after each practice activity and frequently thereafter when they begin working on subject area projects. Some ideas for evaluation:

(1) Everyone fills out a questionnaire or rating form or does a free writing on individual participation as well as the group as a whole.

(2) One person acts as an observer in each group and reports what she saw; members discuss report and what they can do to improve.

(3) Teacher freezes action and asks groups to report their progress to the whole class or to discuss it in their small groups. (If the room gets too noisy, freezing the action is better than telling students to quiet down.)

(4) One group acts as observers for another group. (Each student is assigned to observe one member of the group being evaluated.) Report and discussion follow.

Here are some other suggestions for making small group activities go more smoothly:

(1) Assign students to groups yourself so that you balance abilities and personalities in each.

(2) Make the task specific, set time limits, and give clear directions before students begin working.

(3) If the project will take several days to complete, break the large task down into smaller units so that each group session has a specific objective.

(4) To establish better working relationships and allow groups to build trust, keep the same students together for a period of time. Let students name their groups.

(5) Ask students to rotate the jobs of chair and recorder.

(6) Check on the groups' progress by requiring each group to hand in or present orally a summary of the day's activities at the end of each class period.

(7) If you have any students who simply can't adjust to working in a group, remove them and give alternate individual assignments. Let them try again later if they want to and are willing to make a commitment to cooperate this time.

Besides the fact that small group work encourages students to become more responsible for their own learning and gets them to participate actively in the learning process, small groups can save you time. You won't have to prepare lecture material and you'll have five or six projects or papers to evaluate instead of twenty-five or thirty. Look at the assignments you normally give and see if any of them could be done successfully by students working together in a group. If you train them first, students can work very effectively in small groups.

DEVELOPING A PLAN FOR HANDLING CLASSROOM DISRUPTIONS

Even though you plan your classes to keep students interested and involved, you'll have some students, often for reasons that have nothing to do with you, who will not behave appropriately in class. If you don't figure out in advance what you will do when a student refuses to do the assignment or throws a pen across the room, you may find yourself saying and doing things that make matters worse rather than better.

Many inexperienced teachers, overwhelmed by continuing minor problems in the classroom, send students to the vice-principal because they don't know what else to do. Sending students to the office is the *last* thing you should do, because you're telling the students by your action that you are incapable of handling the situation and must turn to someone else for help. Besides, many students find the office a more interesting place than the classroom. They will misbehave just to see what's going on there, especially if they discover that the vice-principal usually isn't around, doesn't have time to see them, or won't do much anyway. That being the case, these students may continue to act up and hope you will kick them out.

Putting students out in the hall may work the same way, and if a student wanders off while you're busy teaching and gets in trouble elsewhere in the building, you will be held responsible. If you face a major problem (a fight suddenly breaks out or a student comes to your class drunk), you should, of course, immediately send the student(s) to the office or request that someone come to your room. You're much better off figuring out how to handle minor problems yourself. Administrators will love you for not burdening them with extra work, and you'll find that it won't matter much to you (at least as far as discipline in your room is concerned) whether or not the current administration is strong or weak.

One of the keys to better discipline is planning in advance how you will handle problems when they occur. Often teachers get themselves boxed into a corner when frustration with a student or situation causes them to make a threat they can't, can't easily, or shouldn't carry out. "If you do that one more time, John, you'll be out of this class for good!" "One more time and you'll go to the office!" "Stop that talking, Susan. If I have to speak to you one more time, you'll see me after school." "That does it, Sean. You report to me right after school today!"

You may wonder what's wrong with the last example, asking the student to stay after school. Consider what that means. First, you'll have to be there yourself, and if you blurted out the threat without thinking, you may have forgotten about the required faculty meeting today. Even if it's no hardship for you to meet the student today, perhaps he won't show up because of a dental appointment, athletic practice, detention for another teacher, or lack of transportation if he's a bus student. You wouldn't want the class interrupted further if he were to tell you this in the middle of class, and he's not likely (if you made the threat in anger) to stop and tell you after class. So when he doesn't show up, you'll be forced to spend extra time finding out why he didn't come and setting another time. If you don't, then he (and others in the class because word gets around) will know that you don't mean what you say.

Some teachers think they can solve the problem by doubling the time every day a student doesn't show, but all that accomplishes is getting the student so deep in a hole that he can never dig himself out. Usually, the teacher finally has to resort to the vice-principal for help when he finds he is unable to get the student to make up the time. A little problem now escalates into a big problem. If the vice-principal assigns the student to Saturday detention, in-school or out-of-school suspension, the parent must be notified. If the teacher hasn't first called the parent (and many fail to do so), the parent is angry that he wasn't told so he could make sure the student stayed after school in the first place. Of course, the student and the teacher are both unhappy about the situation. The vice-principal, whose workload has been increased unnecessarily, may rightfully question the teacher's ability to handle routine matters of discipline. The whole unpleasant episode could have been avoided with a little advance planning and common sense on the part of the teacher.

If the situation described sounds a little familiar and you'd like to know how to prevent something like that from happening in the future, read on.

First make a plan. Go through the steps listed below.

(1) List as many things as you can think of that students shouldn't do in the classroom.

(2) Separate those which interfere with other students' learning from those that don't. (You don't need to interrupt the class and make an issue when you see a student staring out the window instead of doing homework, although a few private words might be in order.)

(3) Divide the rest into two categories: major and minor. (What you should do about major problems, such as fighting, are probably already covered in the school rules.)

(4) Eliminate from the minor list the ones that don't seem very important or can be handled without a "procedure." (I would never make an issue, for example, of gum chewing. If students chew discreetly and don't leave gum stuck on desks, I usually say nothing. If someone is chomping noisily or blowing bubbles, I make a simple request, keeping my tone of voice pleasant, "Would you please put your gum in the waste-

basket." Many minor things can be dealt with quite easily if you politely request rather than confront students. Don't attach penalties for matters you consider trivial, because that increases the likelihood that a small problem will become a bigger one.)

(5) After you read the rest of this section and the next one, decide how you will handle the others: warnings; consequences; conference with student; time out; contacting parent, guidance counselor, administrator.

(6) Once you have worked out your plan, let students know what it is and stick with it!

TIPS FOR GOOD CLASSROOM CONTROL: FOCUS ON PREVENTION

(1) Act confident (even if you don't feel that way).

(2) Use eye contact when speaking to the class or individuals. (If you won't look directly at students, they may perceive you as weak or afraid.)

(3) Use body language or warning looks for little things instead of interrupting the lesson to say something aloud.

(4) Make a concentrated effort to learn students' names and use them.

(5) Move around the room.

(6) Involve as many students as possible in the class.

(7) If the lesson is question and answer, give the question *before* calling on anyone so they will all mentally prepare an answer. Vary the types of questions you ask: yes, no and one-word answers won't spark much discussion and aren't as interesting to students as questions which make them think.

(8) Keep students busy.

(9) If work has to be written on board during class, have a student do it.

(10) Allow students to work in groups or move freely around the room only when you are sure you have the class well in control.

(11) Keep students from leaving the room unless absolutely necessary and then allow only one student out at a time.

(12) Tell students in class and study hall that no one will get a library pass or other privilege until attendance has been taken and everyone is working quietly.

(13) Give specific directions when asking students to do anything, even just passing in papers.

(14) When problems do occur, follow your plan and *don't* resort to any of the following: threats you can't carry out, punishments which may create greater problems, ultimatums, or punishing the whole class.

(15) Use positive statements to motivate students.

(16) Be understanding, firm, fair, and friendly.

(17) Keep your sense of humor and use it, but avoid sarcasm and humor at the expense of a student, no matter what.

WHAT TO DO ABOUT GENERAL PROBLEMS

When a problem involves many or all of the students in the class, try the following:

(1) Check the physical arrangements and seating in the room to see if the problem can be corrected by changing things or people around. One teacher discovered that a recurring disturbance was due to the fact that students on their way to sharpen a pencil or get additional paper had to walk by a boy who couldn't resist trying to trip anyone who went past. The solution was simple: she moved the offending student. If the pencil sharpener hadn't been involved, too, she might have changed the location of the paper supply instead.

(2) Tell students how you feel about the situation and ask them to tell you in a free writing what they think the problem is, what its causes are, and how the situation might be improved.

(3) Use the information you get from students in the free writings to make changes in the class or to structure further discussion in class. Tell the students what you are doing and why. Again, invite their comments, either orally or in a free writing.

(4) Free writing is also a good strategy to use when the class knows who the culprit is but you don't. Students can give you information without letting others know that they are doing so.

FREE WRITING AS A MEANS OF PREVENTING PROBLEMS

You can avoid many problems entirely by keeping in touch with what students think and feel about the class by periodically asking them to write about specific class activities or just about the class in general. Many students will write down comments they wouldn't say aloud. If you try a new class activity or see that some procedure or assignment seems to be producing too much tension in the class, ask students to share their feelings with you. You can sometimes spot the difficulty and provide explanations or make adjustments to correct it.

Several students in my education class (curriculum and methods) were frustrated and worried because I hadn't specifically said what information they would have to learn. Rather than lecture on what they had read outside of class, I devoted most of the class time to discussions which didn't always stay on the immediate topic. I wanted them to put all the pieces together themselves even though I knew it would take some time. Many of them didn't understand my method and wished I would just tell them what I wanted them to know. When I discovered from reading their free writings about the class that they were uncomfortable (and I wasn't aware of this from the way they behaved in class), I realized that I needed to explain what I was doing so those students who were panicked because they couldn't understand anything and were already worried about doing poorly on the final exam could relax. Even though they may not have agreed that my method was the best one, they could accept it if they understood it. If I hadn't asked them to do the free writing in the first place, I might not have been aware of their feelings until it was too late to do anything about them.

Here's another example of a problem which would have gone undetected had I not asked students to comment on the class discussion in a free writing at the end of class one day. The discussion was lively, students had differing points of view, and everyone was involved. I thought it was a great class. The students handed me their papers as they went out the door, and I talked briefly with Susan about the project she was working on. She was friendly and relaxed as we chatted. Imagine my surprise when later that day I picked up Susan's free writing and read: "Never have I been so humiliated and put down in class so rudely by someone who disagreed with me! I'm a sensitive person and his remarks almost brought me to tears. Never will I open my mouth in this class and risk such rejection again. I don't care about my grade. I'll participate in my own way from now on." For the life of me, I couldn't figure out what comments she was referring to. I hadn't noticed anything out of the ordinary and never would have known she felt that way had she not told me in the free writing. I wrote Susan a long note, spoke to her privately before the next class, and was able to convince her to try again because her comments were valuable and we needed to hear them.

Although things worked out well that time, the experience made me wonder how many times students had other problems that I might have done something about had I known about them. It occurred to me that in Susan's case, several class periods would have passed before I noticed that she wasn't participating and asked her about it. She might have responded generally to my comment but continued to distance herself from the class. Perhaps her lack of involvement in the class discussions would have led to less concern about the class in general and finally a lower grade for the course and a negative feeling about the subject. I imagined how much worse such an experience might have been for a junior high-aged student, whose self-concept is very shaky, and what that might lead to without a teacher's intervention.

Several experiences like the one with Susan had convinced me of the power and value of getting frequent student feedback to improve my teaching effectiveness, prevent problems from occurring, solve the ones that do come up, and establish positive, personal relationships with students even in fairly large classes where time for individual attention is minimal. To encourage students to use this method of communication with me, I invite them to give me free writings whenever they want to and I always respond in some way: a brief comment on the paper itself, a separate note to the student, or a few words with the student before or after class. Responding to what the student has written is important because it shows students that the free writings are meaningful to you. Students won't bother to share what they're thinking if you ignore what they say.

THREE-STEP METHOD FOR SOLVING INDIVIDUAL STUDENT PROBLEMS

If you plan your lessons to interest and involve students, make sure they understand what is expected of them both in terms of behavior and class assignments, give them some responsibilities in the classroom, frequently invite them to comment on how they are doing and how they think the class is going, help them to feel valued and successful, and treat them as young adults, you will find that you really have few problems that require more than the first step described below. This three-step method works well because it is based on the idea that inappropriate behavior or failure to do what's expected or required is not something for which students need to be punished but a problem which needs to be solved.

The First Step: A Private Conversation with the Student

Whatever the problem is—failure to do the required homework or passing notes in class—the first step is discussing the situation with the student privately. Try to find a few minutes during class while other students are writing or reading to talk to the student at your desk or theirs or outside in the hall. If that's not possible, then ask the student to stop by after class. The remark to make when you're exasperated is not, "See me after school," but "Please see me after class."

The purpose of this private conversation is to make sure the student understands what you expect, to give the student an opportunity to tell you what he or she plans to do about the situation, and to inform what you will do if he or she doesn't follow through. If you've had to remind Sara while other students were giving oral book reports not to whisper to her friend who sits in front of her and she does it again, find a time to talk to her alone as soon as you can. Say, "Sara, some students are very nervous about getting up in front of the class to give a book report, and they deserve all the help they can get from their classmates. What were you doing that wasn't very helpful?" Sara will probably reply that she was whispering. "Even quiet whispering can be upsetting to someone who's feeling ill at ease, and it's always rude. I expect that everyone in my class will display good manners and show concern for the feelings of others without my having to remind them. What are you going to do about this?"

Accept any reasonable attempt on Sara's part to state that she will try to improve and then say, "I'm sure you're mature enough to handle this situation by yourself and don't need to get your parents involved. Right?" Sara will, no doubt, agree. "I hope so because if the problem continues, you'll leave me with no choice but to contact your parents. I'd rather not do that, but it's up to you, and I certainly will if this happens again. Is that clear?" You say all this in a reasonable, neutral tone of voice. You're neither castigating nor threatening her. You simply want to clarify the problem, make sure she understands what she has to do, and let her know what you will do if the problem isn't solved.

Depending upon the specific problem, you may wish to try other means to solve it before contacting the parents. For example, in Sara's case, you might say, "I imagine that you like sitting near your friend Jennifer." Sara agrees. You continue, "Well, I'd like to think you're mature enough to sit near her without disturbing the class by talking to her when you both should be listening. I'll give you a chance to show me that you are, but if you're talking again, I'll have to move your seat. You'll make the choice by your future actions. Agreed?" What you're proposing is clear and reasonable and leaves the decision to Sara. If the problem continues, follow through by changing her seat and tell her at that time your next step will be to call her parents. Always let the student know specifically what will happen next, and make it clear that he or she can prevent further consequences by taking care of the problem themselves. When you use this approach, you don't get involved in arguments that upset both of you and rarely produce any positive change.

Another Alternative: Time Out

Some students who are disruptive in class may benefit from time by themselves just to settle down or to come up with a plan for eliminating the undesirable behavior. If you have or can create a private space in your room to use as a time-out area, you can temporarily remove students from the class without sending them to the office or out in the hall. I made such a place by turning the file cabinet sideways in the back corner of the room and moving it out from the wall far enough to make room for a chair where one student could sit and not see or be seen by any of his classmates.

When you assign a student to the time-out area, give him a specific purpose (coming up with a plan) or a specified length of time (10 minutes). Talk with the student privately so that he clearly understands the reason for the action and what he is to do while he is there, e.g. come up with a plan for change, do a free writing on what he thinks is causing the problem, or just take a few minutes away from other students to regain his composure.

Time out will *not* work if the student sees it as punishment, so make every effort to communicate by your words and tone of voice that you are giving him the opportunity to fix things up before they get worse. Time out should normally be limited only to a few minutes or one class period, but Lewis, a hyperactive student in my seventh grade class, needed a full week there before he returned to the class. When previous efforts to get Lewis to stop disrupting the class by such things as talking out of turn and tripping students who walked by his desk failed, I simply said, "Lewis, your behavior is unacceptable. It's keeping others from learning and so far you haven't been successful in correcting it. I guess you just aren't mature enough to be in a class with other students, so from now on you'll be in a class by yourself." I showed him his chair behind the filing cabinet, gave him some work to do, and said, "This will be your classroom until you are ready to join the rest of us. When you can make a commitment to me that you will behave appropriately, let me know."

I didn't call Lewis's parents to explain what I was doing and why, but it's a very good idea to do so. Although there was no problem in Lewis's case, there might have been. It's easy to get involved in a sticky and unpleasant situation if parents hear a distorted version of the events from the student, get angry because the teacher is picking on their child, and call the principal.

A week later Lewis asked me if he could return to his regular seat. Of course, he did not change in one week from a hyperactive, disruptive child into a model student, but he did try to cooperate, and when he had occasional lapses, he did respond to a stern look or a verbal reminder from me. Students like Lewis must be encouraged to continue working on developing more self-control; jumping on them for every little slip short circuits the process.

Unlike Lewis, Robin, a high school sophomore, spent only ten minutes in the time-out area after shouting at another girl in the class and dumping her books on the floor. I asked Robin to do a free writing on what had happened to make her so upset. As it turned out, she wasn't even angry with her victim. Just before she came to class, her boyfriend told her he wanted to break up. As she did the free writing, Robin worked out her feelings of frustration and rejection and was calm and in control when she finished it. She rejoined the class, and I read what she had written and spoke briefly with her at the end of class. On her own, she apologized to the other student and there were no further incidents.

Skip Detention and Schedule Afternoon Appointments

The problem-solving approach is positive, so eliminate the negative word *detention* from your vocabulary. When a student is late to class, making up the time missed is a logical consequence, but for all other problems spending time sitting in a room is probably not effective in solving them. Some students show how they feel about detention by not showing up, forcing you to spend extra time following up. You may want to see students after school because that's the only time you can talk with them privately or give them individual help. If so, tell them why you want to see them, pointing out that it is not a punishment, and call it an afternoon appointment.

Have some slips printed which say "Afternoon Appointment" and carry a notice that students must give you twenty-four hours' notice if they can't keep an appointment. When you explain the procedure, mention that dentists charge for appointments when someone forgets, and that keeping appointments is a responsibility students must take seriously. Certainly emergencies will come up, but they need to let you know before, not after, the fact and reschedule the appointment for another time. Because this approach is positive and parallels real-life experiences, students will usually be more faithful about honoring an afternoon appointment than they ever were about reporting for detention.

APPOINTMENT REMINDER

Date: ____________________

To: ______________________

You have an appointment scheduled with

Mrs. Dodd on ____________________

at ____________ in Room D-7 for

If for any reason you are unable to keep this appointment, please make arrangements <u>before</u> then to re-schedule it.

Figure 10. Afternoon Appointment Reminder Form.

Conversation, Not Confrontation

If you look at disruptive behavior or failure to do assignments as problems to solve rather than personal attacks on you, you can adopt an attitude which encourages students to work with you instead of against you. Forget about punishments and penalties and think in terms of consequences and solutions. When you are dealing with a potentially hostile student, choose your words and monitor your tone very carefully so that the student doesn't react negatively and change what you intended as a conversation into a confrontation. Suppress any feelings of anger or frustration you might have and maintain a calm and pleasant, but firm and serious attitude. Ask questions rather than deliver a lecture. Students know what your rules and expectations are, and when you get the students themselves to restate a rule or requirement, you reinforce its importance without making students feel they're under attack.

For minor matters, such as being late to class or failing to turn in a paper on time, consider this approach. "You didn't get to class on time. What happened?" By first inviting the student to tell you why, you may learn, even from a student who has been late before without a good excuse, that today there was a good reason. If that is the case, then you can say, "I understand the choice you made, but it causes problems for both of us when you are late." (Elaborate on difficulties that can ensue from the student's name being sent to the office on an absence slip or missing an explanation of a homework assignment, etc.) "Is there some other way you could handle this kind of problem next time so you won't be late to class?" The student will probably come up with something. Accept it and say, "I hope this doesn't happen again because if it does, even if you have a good excuse, you will have to make up the time you miss" (or "I will have to call your parents," if that will be your next step). If you treat the student as a responsible young adult, he may become one. In any case, he won't leave thinking you are mean and unfair. Because you have been understanding this time but firm and clear about what you expect in the future, you've increased the chances of solving the problem once and for all.

If a problem is an assignment that hasn't been completed on time, ask questions such as, "Why didn't you do your assignment?" "What is the penalty for handing in a late assignment in this class?" "What are you going to do about the missing work?" Before the conversation ends, get the student to tell you when he will finish the work and give it to you. Remind him what will happen if he fails to live up to his commitment and follow through, if necessary. In most cases the student will do the work as promised, saving you the trouble of taking further action.

The same approach also works for more serious problems like cheating. If you get test papers from two students with the same unusual errors, get the students together at a time when you can talk in private. Show them the tests, point out the suspicious errors, and ask, "What would you think if you were I?" The students will probably say that you will think they cheated but deny that they did. Don't accuse or contradict them; just ask, "How do you suppose you both ended up putting down such unlikely wrong answers?"

When you use the problem-solving approach, it doesn't matter that crimes are punished. What you want is a resolution to the immediate situation and some indication that it won't happen again. You don't have to force the culprits to admit their misdeeds as long as they get the message so they won't do it again. If you can see that they won't admit to cheating, move on. "I can't feel comfortable giving you the grades for these tests because of these answers. Do you have any ideas about what I might do?" The students will probably suggest a makeup test or the three of you can come to an agreement on another solution.

After you've clarified what will be done in this case, tell the students that if you get tests with answers like these from them again, you won't give them any credit and you will contact their parents. You'll probably never have to speak to them again. The fact that you didn't accuse and berate them will make them want to do the right thing next time. Even though you didn't say it and they didn't admit it, you all understand that they did cheat this time. They didn't get away with anything.

On the other hand, confronting and/or punishing students may not only fail to solve the initial problem but instead create bigger ones. After the teacher in a high school creative writing class told students they could write anything they wanted in their journals, she received from one girl in the class a journal filled with descriptions of explicit sex and plenty of obscene language. The teacher was shocked and disappointed. When she spoke to the girl about the journal, the conversation turned in to a confrontation. The student maintained that the teacher had told the class that the journals were theirs, so if she wanted to write stuff like that, she could. The teacher got upset because she felt the girl was challenging her authority and ended up not resolving anything but instead setting up a power struggle which affected the whole class. As it turned out, the girl had the power to turn other students in the class against the teacher, and soon nearly everyone was involved in sabotaging everything the teacher did.

The situation could have been avoided if the teacher had swallowed her authoritarian pride and instead asked the student for help in figuring out how they could work out a compromise. The following questions would be helpful in this regard: "What would your mother think if she read this and knew I was giving you credit for it?" "How can I justify this kind of writing to my department head or principal?" "Are there some things you can say and do in private that aren't okay in public?" "Would you consider school a public or a private place?" Even if the student had written the journal solely for the purpose of seeing how the teacher would react, a conversation based on the questions above might make the student reconsider the wisdom of her action and perhaps improve her relationship with the teacher.

If all else failed, the teacher could say without confronting the student, "I know I said the journal was yours, but I was wrong. Since it is a class assignment, it is yours but with certain restrictions. You may keep a really private journal at home and write whatever you want, but for your class journal, you'll have to avoid the kind of material you've written here. Thank you for helping me realize that I must be more careful in the future when I explain this assignment. Can we agree?" In all but the most extreme cases, the student would agree. If she didn't, then that's the point at which the teacher probably needs to involve someone else—the parent, a guidance counselor, or an administrator.

The Second Step: Contacting Parents

If a student does not respond to your first efforts to get him to solve the problem on his own and you have told him the next step is contacting his parents, you must do that or lose your credibility. After word gets around that you've called a few parents, other students may suddenly develop more self-discipline and save you the time and trouble of calling theirs. Because the fewer students you have causing problems, the less energy and effort you'll have to waste, the time you spend calling parents even when you have to do it on your own time at home will be worth it. If calling parents is a toll call from your home, ask the principal if you can bill such calls to the school. If you point out that your calling the parent will probably make his job easier (if you solve the problem, he'll never have to bother with it), he'll be more likely to approve. But if the answer is no, try getting to school early so you can reach parents before they go to work.

When you call the parent, remember that your goal is to solve the problem. Ninety-nine percent of the parents will be responsive and helpful, but don't despair if you get one of the remaining one percent who gets angry when you call and fills your ear with criticisms about the lousy school and its incompetent and unfair teachers and your failure to understand their perfect-but-misunderstood child. If you're having a hard time dealing with the child, ten to one the parents are, too. All the parents' noise is probably an effort to ventilate their own frustrations with the child and has little to do with you. If that's the case, simply state as briefly as you can what the problem is and that you'd appreciate any help the parent can give. If the parent becomes more rational after the initial blowup, begin at the beginning as described next. If not, thank her for her time and hang up. Your next step with that child will involve the guidance counselor and administrators. You will have gained some valuation information, however. Knowing the child's home environment will probably cause you to redouble your own efforts to reach him or her at school.

When you have the parent on the line, introduce yourself and say something like, "I'm sorry to bother you. Is this a convenient time for you to talk for a few minutes? (If not, arrange another time or ask if the parent can call you back.) I've been having a problem with Johnny which I have been unable to resolve, and I'd really appreciate your help. Maybe if we both work on it, we can figure out a way to solve it. (Explain the problem and what steps you've already taken. Give the parent time to respond and discuss the issues. Come to some agreement about what you will do, what the parent will do, and what Johnny will do. Repeat the agreed-upon plan to make sure you and the parent have the same understanding.) I certainly hope this plan works, Mrs. Smith, because I know it would be difficult for you to come in for a conference at school. But if the problem continues, we'll have to sit down with the principal (vice-principal or guidance counselor) to see what else we can try. I certainly appreciate your time and help on this. Thank you."

You'll notice that you should outline the next step for the parent in the same way you do it when you talk with the student. Check with the student the next day and make sure he knows that the next step in this case will be a conference at school. As soon as you've made the call, write a note in your grade book about it, include the date, and briefly indicate what you talked about. If you promised to let the parent know how the student was doing in a week or two, put a big note on your calendar to call or send a note. All your efforts so far will be wasted if you don't follow through and follow up. You'll not only lose credibility, but you can do great damage to the relationship between school and home by promising something you fail to deliver. For this reason you might want to consider leaving the parent with the responsibility to get in touch with you to see how Johnny's doing in a few weeks instead of the other way around. The parent only has two or three children to worry about, while you probably have a hundred or more.

If you have any reason to think the phone call to the parent might not solve the problem, take a few minutes to let the principal (or vice-principal) and guidance counselor (special education teacher, too, if that applies) know what you've done and why and that you told the parent the next step would be a conference. They will appreciate knowing what you've done in case the student has difficulties with another teacher, and they'll have some advance notice that you may want them to sit in on a conference with the parent should that become necessary. Nothing is more frustrating for a teacher than not having administrative support when it's needed. If you inform administrators in advance and let them know what you may need from them in the future, they'll be there when you need them. The few minutes it takes to stop the principal in the hall or drop him a note can save you hours of frustration and aggravation later.

The Third Stage: Conference with Parents

Up to this point, you've been handling the problem by yourself and you may wish to schedule this meeting with the parents that way, too. Chances are, however, since the original problem still hasn't been solved, you will need help from others in the school to solve it now. Once you decide what the best approach will be, contact the parents and set a time when they will come to school to meet with you. If the principal or guidance counselor will be there, too, either one will probably take care of setting up a meeting. Invite the student for part or all of the conference, where once again the focus is on finding a way to solve the problem.

After the group develops a plan, remember that you're the adult most directly involved, so make sure that eveyone understands who's to do what, when and what happens if the plan doesn't work. Any discipline problem that goes unresolved after this point should involve someone else in the school. Perhaps the student needs to be tested for special placement, moved to another class, or disciplined by the administrators. You've done all you can. Take heart, though. Very few problems ever get this far. The first two steps are so effective at solving problems that you may never need this one at all.

A FINAL WORD

If you've never tried a problem-solving approach to discipline, you may have been punishing yourself needlessly with after-school detentions and unpleasant and unproductive encounters with students. This method reduces student hostility and allows them to make choices so you really aren't doing anything to them. By knowing the consequences of their choices in advance, they are doing it to themselves. If students get frustrated, they have themselves to blame, not you. You're also teaching them that they have the power to control events by controlling their own behavior. For helping students become more reasonable and productive, this method's hard to beat, and the best part is that by spending some extra time talking with students and calling parents at the beginning of the year, you'll avoid an incredible amount of time and stress later.

CHAPTER FIVE

GRADING WITHOUT GRIEF

Mr. Griffin unburdens himself to a colleague in the teacher's room. "I'd like to get rid of grades! The last week of the quarter all I heard was 'What can I do for extra credit?' 'What's my average?' and 'What do I have for makeup?' That drove me crazy, but this week is even worse. One of my students pleaded with me to change her grade so her parents could get the 'good student discount' on their auto insurance! Then this lazy kid who didn't do one assignment on time all quarter and failed three out of four exams accused me of flunking him because I didn't like him! He told me I'd be sorry because his father, some VIP, is going straight to the principal. There MUST be an easier way to earn a living!"

ONCE AGAIN, advance planning is the key to making the necessary but unpleasant task of correcting student work and determining quarter grades less onerous. If you figure out what you'll use as a basis for student grades at the same time you do your planning for the unit or marking period, you can save yourself a great deal of stress. Students, too, will benefit. They'll be motivated to work harder when they understand from the outset just what you expect and how much each assignment counts. You can further increase their motivation by including options for earning meaningful extra credit and by involving them in the process of assigning quarter grades.

A BASIC PRINCIPLE FOR REDUCING THE NUMBER OF FAILURES

On the first day of class, anounce to students that no one will pass the course unless they complete *every* assignment. Before you dismiss this idea as totally unworkable because you're sure your students would revolt if you made such a pronouncement or you'd have more failure rather than less, read on. This method works extremely well if you make your expectations clear to students in the beginning, commit yourself to the follow-up which will be necessary for some students, and follow through by failing those students who don't complete everything.

When you make your announcement, someone will protest, "That's not fair. How can you fail us for missing one homework assignment?" You reply, "Some of you may have a very difficult time with this subject and I want you to know that I will guarantee you a passing grade, at least a D–, even if you do poorly on tests and quizzes as long as you show me that you are making an effort. The way you show me that you are trying is to do all of the assignments as well as you can. All the work I want you to do is important. If I were to average grades, a bright student who can easily get A's on tests might decide to skip the term paper and still end up with a C in the course, while those of you who are not so capable could spend hours on the paper and, because of lower test grades, end up with a D in the course. I don't think that's fair, so if you care about getting a passing grade, you'll do all the assignments. If you miss a couple of assignments, I'll assume that you don't care and you won't pass. It wouldn't be fair if I were to do this without telling you first, but now that you all understand the ground rules, you can make the decision."

Your students may not believe you at first and you may have to prove that you mean business by actually giving an F for the marking period to a student who was only missing a couple of homework assignments. The first time I tried this method I thought that might happen and I was prepared to do what I said, but in the many years since, no one has ever challenged me. The students who did fail were those who were absent a great deal, had a number of missing assignments, and would have failed regardless of the method I used to determine grades.

Be forewarned, however. There is some extra work involved at first. You'll have to remind some students that they have back work to turn in. The easiest way to handle the situation is to set a final deadline for makeup work one week before the marking period ends. As you record quiz or other grades in your grade book, jot notes to students who have work due at the tops of the papers you're returning. Stop them as they come in to the room and mention the missing assignments to them. Put the deadline for back work on your calendar assignment sheet and write it in a prominent place on the chalkboard. (Near the end of the quarter you may also list names of delinquent students, too.) Although I reminded students that they have work to complete in a number of ways throughout the quarter, I also made up a small form on which I listed the missing assignments to give to individual students near the makeup deadline. If there was a student who owed quite a bit of work, I also called the student's parent, explained the grading policy, noted what the student still had to do, and made sure the parents knew when the deadline was and what the penalty would be if the student failed to meet it. But make this call early enough so that the student has time to do the work. It's amazing how industrious some students suddenly become once their parents find out they've been slacking off.

A REMINDER about

Your Missing Assignments

Date: ______________________

To: ______________________

According to my records, you have not turned in the following assignments:

DON'T MISS THE DEADLINE INDICATED ON YOUR ASSIGNMENT CALENDAR!

Figure 11. Missing Assignments Reminder Form.

What I've outlined above may sound like a great deal of extra work. It really isn't. In the first place when students see that you mean business (and they can tell that by your constant, if casual, reminders), most will not get behind. The few who will fail are the ones who would cause you extra work no matter what system you used. You may feel that you shouldn't have to take the time to remind them of missing work. I do it because I think junior high and high school students aren't always mature enough to make the best choices on their own and also because I want them and their parents to know that how well students do in the course is largely up to them. The beauty of this plan is that it places the responsibility for passing or not passing squarely on the students' shoulders. Since they can control their own fate, they can't put the blame for their poor grades on the teacher.

I invite you to try the method and assess its results. In case you have a hard-nosed student or two you have to fail for the quarter to make your point, plan to use the method for at least two quarters. I think you'll be amazed at the difference it can make in your classes. One math teacher who was continually frustrated because several students came to class without having done their homework made his own problem worse by giving students time at the beginning of class to complete the work whenever he discovered that several students did not have it done. Of course, this practice led to more students who didn't do the homework. Why should they bother working outside of class when they knew they would have time the next day in class? At first he was hesitant to try this approach which sounded very risky, but when other methods failed to solve the problem he created, he finally did. It worked. Not only was he able to get more accomplished during the class time, but he was also surprised to discover that the few students who needed extra reminding were the same ones who didn't finish the work even when they had been given time in class. One quarter later even most of these students were working because they had discovered they had some power to decide what grades they would get.

THE HOMEWORK GRADE

The method described above gets students to do all the homework by the end of the marking period; the homework grade encourages students to do homework on time. In most classes teachers do not want to grade homework, since much of it is practice or preliminary work, and some students may have difficulty understanding what they're supposed to be doing until the teacher has spent more class time working with them. If that description fits your concept of homework, then all you're concerned about is whether or not the student did spend some time on the assignment. The homework is either done or it's not.

Before the quarter begins, decide what percentage of the quarter grade will be based on homework and tell the students the first day, "Ten percent of your quarter grade is for homework. Right now you all have an A for the ten percent. You can keep that A just by doing the best you can on each assignment and having your paper ready in class at the beginning of the period to be checked. If you're absent, you have one day for each day you were out to make up the work without penalty. However, if you come in to class without your homework one day, your homework grade will drop to a B and you will continue to lose one letter grade each day until the work is handed in. I already said that you would pass if you did every assignment by the makeup deadline and that's true, but the passing grade I guarantee is a D–, not a B or a C. Remember, you already have an A for ten percent of your quarter grade. All you have to do now is keep it."

Because this is a positive approach to grading homework, many students will respond immediately. You'll find that the students who are difficult to motivate because they have met with failure after failure since they've been in school will often surprise you by doing the homework without complaint. It makes a big difference when students have a little power to control their own destinies.

Of course, you do have to check the homework everyday and keep accurate records of when students turn work in late, or the "system" will self-destruct. You can check to see that students have papers by walking around the room, grade book in hand, at the beginning of the period (or delegate the task to a student). Put a dot (period) in the square in your grade book for the day's homework if students do not have a paper, a check for complete work, and a check minus if the work is done but carelessly or incompletely. The dot shows you that the homework grade has been reduced. When students do hand in a back assignment, write the date down beside the dot. That's all the information you need to figure out what the homework grade should be later when you do your grades for the quarter. (When my students learned about the dots that indicates late papers, I acquired a new nickname, "Mrs. Dott.")

WHAT STUDENTS CAN DO FOR EXTRA CREDIT

Some students will get behind and may not want to do much work if all they'll get is a D– for the quarter. To keep them motivated and make it possible for them to recoup some of their early losses before the end of the marking period, provide several options for extra credit. Set a deadline for accepting extra credit (perhaps the same date as that for turning in back work) and tell students that extra credit must be done as they go along. You will not accept a large stack of extra credit at the end of the quarter just because they got worried about their grades at the last minute. You can probably come up with other ways students in your class can do meaningful extra work in addition to those listed below.

(1) Rewrite essays, reports, research papers.

(2) Rewrite responses to essay questions on tests.

(3) Respond in a free writing to optional outside reading in books and magazines.

(4) Respond in a free writing to course-related TV programs.

(5) Write a summary of the material covered in a test.

(6) Do a class assignment again on another topic.

(7) Do something creative with material studied in class, e.g. writing a short story, children's book, poem, or play or making a poster, collage, or mobile.

(8) Research some topic related to course and report orally to class.

(9) Interview someone in the community on a topic related to what's being studied and report findings to class.

All of the suggestions listed involve the students actively with course material. Rewriting essays and answers to essay questions will help them improve their skills and do better on similar assignments in the future. Note that free writings and oral reports are suggested for outside reading and research. These activities are likely to encourage real learning because they force students to think about what they read and to respond in their own words, thus avoiding having them waste time and effort by going to the library and copying information from an encyclopedia, an activity of questionable educational value. (If you want to know more about using writing as a tool for learning, see the section, "Writing Across the Curriculum" in the Bibliography.)

COLLABORATIVE GRADING WITH THE STUDENT GRADE SHEET

Collaborative grading, that is, teacher and student working together to decide on the quarter grade, is a way of eliminating arguments with students and the hard feelings and stress that result from these unpleasant confrontations at report card time. The student grade sheet provides a way to avoid both these hassles and the late nights and weekends spent averaging grades at home four times a year.

The grade sheet is nothing more than a dittoed form on which the student keeps a record throughout the quarter of grades, makeup and extra work, along with the dates work was completed. When you explain the grade sheet to students, say, "You are to keep this sheet in your notebook. When you turn graded assignments in, list them and the dates on the sheet. When I return your papers and tests to you, record the grades. Note when and what you do for makeup or extra work as well. When I check your notebooks to determine your notebook grade (see Chapter Four), you will lose credit if your grade sheet is not up-to-date. What's even more important though is that the grade sheet will allow you to have some say in determining your own grade at the end of the quarter. I will ask you to answer the questions at the bottom of sheet about class participation and attendance, average your own grades, and turn these sheets in. I will then compare the grade you think you should get with the one I have penciled in my grade book. If the two grades are different, I will reconsider mine in light of the evidence you present on your grade sheet. In some cases I'll change my grade. If I don't, I'll sit down with you and see if we can come to an agreement on the grade. BUT, and this is the catch, if you haven't kept your grade sheet throughout the quarter, you'll have to take the grade I give you, I won't discuss your grade with you, and you'll have to wait until report cards come out to find out what you got."

Most students will quickly see how advantageous keeping up with the grade sheet will be to them. And you may be surprised when you see their completed grade sheets to find that students are generally tougher on themselves than you would be. By using this method and setting up your grades in categories by weight (see the next section on the grade book for details), you won't have to average numbers to arrive at a letter grade for the quarter. You can simply read across the lines and pencil in a letter. The students will average their own grades, so you can avoid doing any math except for the ones where there is a discrepancy. As you go through the student grade sheets, write the final grades on which you and the students agree in ink. Return the grade sheets to students whose grades are all set and take time in class while students are working on an assignment to have conferences with students whose grades do not agree with your own. After you talk with these students, ink-in their grades as well.

Course ________________ Period __ Quarter __ Name ________________

KEEP THIS SHEET UNTIL THE END OF THE QUARTER. NO GRADES WILL BE DISCUSSED IF YOU HAVE NOT COMPLETED AND TURNED IN THIS FORM.

GRADED ASSIGNMENTS (Keep a list of checked assignments and free writings with dates on the back of this sheet.)

Date	Assignment	Grade	Rewritten/Corrected (Date)

1. How many assignments have you handed in late? (List with dates.)

2. How much have you contributed to class discussions? Explain what you did.

3. How valuable were your contributions to small group activities? Did you do your fair share of the group work?

4. How often did you waste time in class?
   in small groups?

5. What extra work have you done for this course?

6. How many times were you absent? ___ tardy? ___

My quarter grade for this course should be ___ because ... (Finish the statement. Use the back of the sheet, if necessary.)

Figure 12. Sample of a Student Grade Sheet.

Even when students hope for higher grades than you are willing to give, they will usually accept what they get after hearing your explanation and having an opportunity to discuss the situation with you. By having these private talks about grades in advance of the report cards, you can also avoid upsetting calls from parents, too, since most of the students who aren't doing well are smart enough to prepare their parents ahead of time and, after all your efforts, they will be unlikely to blame you for their low grades with such claims as "She doesn't like me" or "He's unfair and flunks everyone."

The grade sheet also involves students in determining what they should get for a class-participation grade. Teachers want to grade class participation, but many find it difficult to come up with an objective means of doing so. Although this method is still subjective, the student, not the teacher, must come up with a grade and support it. All you have to do is approve or disapprove of what the student chooses and discuss it.

THE RANK BOOK: A RECORD OF GRADES AND MORE

In addition to grades, use your rank book to record any information which may be useful to you in the future. Since most of the time when you will be contacting parents you'll want to refer to grades and attendance information which are already there, the rank book is a good place to list parents' names, phone numbers and addresses. In the back of the book or in the comment space next to a student's name, jot down a note to remind you when you made a phone call or sent a note to a parent and what it was about.

You should also note the date you sent warning notices to students. It's good public relations to keep parents informed, and some schools have a policy that a teacher may not fail a student if a warning was not given previously. Should some parent, whose child may have intercepted all communications from the school, complain to the principal at a later date, you'll have documentation right at hand. Your rank book record may be enough to save you from sorting through piles of paper looking for a copy of a warning notice to prove that you did issue one even though the parent never received it.

The back of the rank book is a good place for other information to which you may want to refer. Keep a record of the conferences you have with parents, the date, and what was discussed. Record the dates, times, and what was happening in class when the principal or department head came in observe your classes. You may also want to set aside a few pages for listing the names of the students in your classes and their report card grades for the year. If you have to hand in your grade book at the end of the year and will not get it back (as is the procedure in some schools), you can tear these pages out and have a permanent record of the students you taught. It also puts the grades for quarters and semesters all together in one place so you can easily arrive at a semester or year average if that information is required on the report cards.

Organizing Grades in the Rank Book

After you have planned your lessons for the marking period and have decided on the weight for each assignment, plan the spaces in your rank book to match your lesson plans. Set aside enough space (one square per assignment) to cover all the days students will have written homework which must be checked, but leave a space for the actual homework grade with other assignments that carry a great deal of weight, such as class-participation and notebook grades. Consider leaving space for summarizing some grades, quizzes and minor tests, for example. When all the information you need for averaging grades is grouped together along with the percentage each category is worth, you can do an accurate job of reading across the lines to determine grades instead of working them out mathematically.

Look at the Figure 13 here and consider adapting it to your own classes. If up to now you have used a square in your rank book for every day in the quarter and recorded grades for assignments on the days they occurred, then you must have spent unnecessary time sorting the grades out or doing the math for every quarter grade you assigned.

OTHER TIPS: If your class is small enough so that you write students' names on every other line without going to a second page, do so. You'll have room between the rows of grades to make notes about special circumstances. If you list absences and tardies on your seating charts, simply add these up at the end of the quarter and record the total numbers in your grade book beside the final quarter grade. If your school requires a grade in effort/behavior, ask students to tell you what grades they should get and why; then use the same collaborative process you used for class-participation and quarter grades in the course. To make sure you don't overlook any missing assignments near the end of the quarter before the makeup deadline, take a red pen and circle all the squares where assignments are missing so that they stand out. When students hand in work, you'll fill the empty, red-circled squares with check marks or grades and the date work was completed.

Ancient History Period 4 Quarter 3

	2/4 H.W	2/11 H.W	3/4 H.W	3/18 H.W	4/8 H.W	Home-work Grade	2/12 Quiz #1	2/26 Quiz #2	3/23 Exam #1	4/18 Exam #2	4/11 Term Project	Abs.	NOTES Quarter Grade
Alexander	✓	✓	✓	✓	✓	A	C	B	B	B-	B-	2	B
Canton	✓	✓	✓	✓	✓	A	A-	A-	B+	A-	A-	0	A-
Darcy	✓	✓	✓	✓	✓	A	A	A	A	A	A	0	A
Fenwick	✓•	✓•	✓	✓•	(✓•)	D-	C	D	F	D-	D	3	D-
Fisher	✓	✓	✓	✓	✓	A	B	C	C+	C-	C	1	C+
Hill, C.	✓	✓•	✓	✓	✓	A-	B	C	B+	B-	B-	0	B-
Hill, J.	✓	✓	✓	✓	✓	A	A	A	A	A	A-	0	A
Harrison	(•)	(•)	✓	(•)	✓	F	D	B	F	F	(•)	8	(F)
Hopkins	✓	✓	✓	✓	✓	A	B	B-	B	B	C+	2	B
Lassey	✓	✓	✓	✓	✓	A	B+	B+	C	A	B+	1	B
Lowell	✓	✓	✓	✓•	✓	B	C-	D	C+	C+	C+	2	C+
Morris	✓	✓	✓	✓	✓	A	B-	B-	B+	D+	B-	2	B-
Novak	✓	✓	✓	✓	✓	A	A-	A-	B+	B+	B	1	B+
O'Brien	✓	✓	✓	✓	✓	A	A-	B+	A-	A-	A	0	A-
Ramone	✓•	✓•	✓	✓	✓	C	D	C+	C+	C+	C	1	C
Parris	✓	✓	✓	✓	✓	A	B+	B+	B+	B+	B	0	B+
Rosinell	✓	✓	✓	✓	✓	A	C	C	C	C	C	0	C+
Velazquez	✓	✓	✓	✓	✓	A	A	B+	B+	B-	B	2	B+
White	✓	✓	✓	✓	✓	A	D	D-	D	D	C-	0	D+
Wilson	✓	✓	✓	✓	✓	A	B+	B-	A-	B-	B	0	B
Williams	✓	✓	✓	✓	✓•	A-	C	C	A-	B-	B-	0	B-

Group grades in categories to make figuring out quarter grades easier.

Figure 13. Sample Rank Book Page.

Ending the Quarter Early: To avoid overload at end of the marking period, consider closing your grades one week earlier than the official end. The work students do during the "real" last week can be counted on the next quarter's grade. This way, instead of rushing to get everything done all at once, you have an extra week to tie up loose ends, figure out grades, and confer with students. Be sure to explain to students what you're doing and why. Of course, you can't use this strategy for the last quarter of the year, but even then you can make sure your big assignments are due earlier than the last week, and since most students' overall grades won't be changed by a few minor assignments, you can go through the process of doing your final grades and going over them with the students before the year ends. Tell students that the grades you decide on, however, are tentative and will be reconsidered if they do not fulfill their responsibilities until the last day of class.

ALTERNATIVES TO GIVING LETTER GRADES FOR ALL ASSIGNMENTS

You can use student contracts or point systems for all or part of a quarter as a substitute for grading individual student work. The students decide what grades they wish to earn by choosing from a variety of assignments. Of course, the high grades go to the students who do more work. Every contract should contain a clause stating that all work completed must meet minimum standards which you will specify. Then if students are tempted to carelessly do a great quantity of work for an easy A, you don't have to accept it.

Decide first what basic assignments everyone must complete, and make these the requirements for a C. Then, add options which vary in weight from which students may choose activities and projects to bring their grades up to B or A. Anyone who doesn't meet the basic requirements will get a D or F. You can list specific activities students must do for a B or A, or you can specify the points needed to earn each grade and provide a list of options with the number of points each is worth from which students can select the ones they wish to do.

Make up a contract form which students complete, telling you what grade they are contracting for and what they will do to earn it. They should keep a running list of what they accomplish and keep all work in a folder. At the end of the contract period (which may be a week, the duration of a unit, or the whole quarter), ask students to check their contract requirements, their completed work, and write a letter to you indicating what their grade should be. Then follow the procedure suggested earlier for meeting with students to discuss their grades.

The contract method works well with lower ability student. You can provide additional motivation by including some activities which are fun, such as doing crossword and math puzzles, but don't let these count too much or you may find students who will spend all their time on puzzles and ignore the basic requirements they must complete.

CONTRACT FOR CREATIVE WRITING

Minimum requirements for a C:

1. Keep a journal--three (3) ten-minute entries per week.
2. Complete all other assignments on time. (If you are absent, you have one day for each day you were out to make up the work you missed.)
3. Participate in a positive manner on a regular basis in class and small group activities.
4. Complete one term project.

Requirements for a B:

1. Keep a journal--four (4) ten-minute entries per week.
2. Complete all other requirements listed for a C.
3. Complete a second term project.

Requirements for an A:

1. Keep a journal--five (5) or more ten-minute entries per week.
2. Complete all other requirements listed for a C
3. Complete a second term project and other additional work discussed and agreed upon with the teacher. The extra work necessary can come from enlarging the scope or depth of one or both of the term projects rather than doing a third one.

I, ______________________________ , contract for a grade of ____ in Creative Writing. I understand that if the work I turn in is not carefully and thoughtfully done, the teacher reserves the right to require that I do it over before accepting it.

For my term project(s) I tentatively plan to do the following:

Date ________________ Signed ________________________

Figure 14. An example of a student contract.

CORRECTING PAPERS IN CLASS

Some teachers get frustrated having students correct papers in class either because they do a poor job or it takes forever to answer all the questions that come up: "Is it wrong if . . . ?" "Should I take off for . . . ?" "Is this answer worded okay?" A similar problem with questions often occurs when teachers go over a test which they have already corrected: "I had the answer right and you marked it wrong." "Why isn't it right?"

The solution is quite simple. Don't answer questions. Anticipate what students might ask about and give examples of acceptable alternative wording when you give the answers. Tell students if they have any questions about an answer (either because they aren't sure whether to mark the answer wrong on a paper they're correcting or because they think a right answer has been marked wrong on their own paper by you or another student) to put a question mark next to that item on the paper and a question mark at the top of the paper. You'll look at the papers and items with question marks later and let them know what you decide.

To encourage more careful correcting by students of their classmates' papers, don't always have the same people correcting each other's papers every time. Ask students to sign the papers they correct and warn that they may be charged for errors they make in correcting by having points deducted from their own grades. (You probably won't have to do this and wouldn't want to if a student makes a careless mistake in correcting. The announcement itself, however, will make students take their responsibilities more seriously.)

MAKEUP MADE EASIER

Some of the strategies you can use to make makup easier have already been mentioned elsewhere in the book. They are listed again here along with a few other tips.

(1) Put a box with a sign that says "Makeup" in a specific place in your room. Empty it after each class and put the papers in your folder for that class. Tell students the box is for routine papers only. They must hand major projects and papers to you personally.

(2) Assign a student to write the "minutes" of each class in the class log, collect copies of handouts, and write the names of absentees on them, making sure that when these students return they get the handouts and check the log to see what else they missed.

(3) Give students calendar assignment sheets for each marking period or unit and require that they keep them in their notebooks. If you have to contact a parent about a student's work, explain the calendar assignment sheet, offer to send them a copy, and ask if they will help out with reminders and reinforcement at home.

(4) Schedule regular help/makeup sessions after school one or two days a week. Schedule students for "afternoon appointments" if they get behind in their work or need individual help with the assignments. Invite all students to drop in on their own.

(5) Set a deadline for handing in back work each quarter one week before you close grades. Tell students that all work must be completed by that date or they will not pass.

(6) Instead of making up another objective quiz or test for students who didn't take the test when the rest of the class did, ask them to respond to an essay question(s). Since these tests require less time to construct, you can give each student a different exam. If the makeup tests are a little more difficult than the ones given in class, students will be less likely to stay out of school on the day a test is scheduled.

TIME-SAVING AND PAPER-FREE EVALUATION TECHNIQUES

Either/Or

If your students are working on a project or assignment which is being done in several stages but won't be formally graded until it's completed, ask students to bring in notes, outlines, rough drafts, and so forth for an intermediate grade—either A (if they can show you the work) or F (if they bring in nothing). Use this method anytime your objective is making sure the students' work is in progress. It encourages students not to wait until the night before to do the whole project; thus, the finished products should be of better quality and more enjoyable to grade than those that come like the overnight express package!

Oral Quiz—Discussion

Check students' understanding of a discussion topic and motivate everyone to participate by giving an "oral quiz." Appoint a student to lead the discussion, using questions from the book or a study guide as a starting point. State the ground rules: (1) No one is to dominate the discussion. (2) A person must participate to receive a passing grade. Then you sit in the back of the room with a class list, marking positive contributions (+), especially thoughtful or insightful comments (*), and negative behavior (–), if there is any, next to students' names. You can interrupt the discussion when necessary to clarify points, correct misunderstandings, or put a student who's dominating on hold. (That student doesn't contribute again until he/she is taken off hold.) At the end of the discussion you assign letter grades by making a scale based on the number and type of contributions each student made. Everyone with at least one contribution passes; use your judgment about the value of the other grades.

Oral "Written Composition"

If your main purpose in assigning a written composition or report is to have the students focus on organization and development of ideas, have them write neat final copies of the paper to turn in for you to check, but grade them only on the content by having them read their papers orally to the class. Make sure you require a neatly written final copy, however. Since many students get little practice reading aloud, the results of their reading from a messy draft could be disasterous. Having them "double-space" their handwriting on the final copy will also facilitate reading. (This is a good idea for the papers you have to grade as well, and when students double-space on rough drafts, they have room to make changes and corrections.)

Book Review Conference

Instead of having students do oral or written book reports, hold conferences with individual students to discuss the books they've read. If you schedule a few every week, you can talk with students while the rest of the class is working on another assignment or continuing to read their own books. This method will eliminate the possibility of students getting credit for reading books they didn't actually read. They will find it very difficult or impossible to respond to your questions in person if they have only the book jacket information to go on.

One-Page Grade

When students write papers longer than two pages, read the whole paper for content, but mark mechanical errors on one randomly chosen page. Choose a different page to check each time so students won't proofread only the page they think you'll read.

Student Choice

If students are writing several papers or reports during the quarter, have them turn in all of them for you to check, but ask them to choose the one (or two) they want graded and put it on top. In a writing class you can ask students to keep all of their writing in a folder. You check the folder to see that all of the work has been done, but grade only the pieces the students have selected for that purpose.

Group Assignment/Essay

If your students frequently work in small groups, give the group a written assignment—a paragraph or short essay to write, questions to answer, or whatever. The group turns in one paper on which everyone in the group is graded. In a class of twenty-five students five groups of students would produce five papers—twenty less for you to grade than if they did individual papers. Students are also learning another very important skill in this process: working cooperatively with others. While the groups are working, you can circulate, checking to see that one or two people in the group are not doing all the work.

One-Question Reading Quiz

Did the students read the assignment last night? Develop one-question quizzes which can't be answered unless they read the whole assignment (or remembered a very detailed summary provided by a friend). Grading is easy—A or F, pass or fail. Students won't easily guess what your one question will be, so they'll have to read the whole assignment. Be sure your question doesn't require much interpretation and isn't too picky. You don't want to punish or trap the students, just make sure they do their homework.

Oral Quiz

Instead of having students write answers to a number of questions on a topic or chapter, give the questions as an oral quiz. Go around the room, giving each student a different question to answer. If a student misses a question, it goes to the next person. If you have enough questions, you can base grades on the percentage right out of the total and assign a letter grade. Of course, pass/fail is another option.

A variation of the oral quiz makes a great game for reviewing material. Organize the activity like a spelling bee, using questions to answer instead of words to spell.

One-Skill-Only Grade

If you're teaching something which requires more than one skill, grade the paper on one skill only, perhaps the one you've been emphasizing most recently. For example, if students have a story to write and you've been working with them on punctuation of dialogue, let the mechanics grade on the story reflect only punctuation of dialogue, nothing else. You can give a separate grade for content. On a math paper which includes problems requiring addition, subtraction, multiplication, and division, grade only division one time. Next time you might grade only addition.

Free-Writing Summary

Have students write free writings to summarize class discussions or chapters they're read in the textbook, respond to a film, or explain the process they are using to solve a problem. Collect them, read them quickly, and check them off in your grade book or invite a few students to read theirs aloud to the class or to others in a small group. You can get a quick idea of how much students have understood or what they misunderstand from those short papers without correcting them. Write a brief comment on each paper so that students will know that you did read them.

Holistic Scoring for Essays, Reports, and Term Projects

Read through the whole set of papers quickly, making no marks on them. As you finish each paper, put it with papers of similar quality by creating the piles as you go along. (This method won't work unless you can do the whole set of papers at one time.) When you've finished all the papers, read through the individual piles, each of which will probably only contain five to seven papers or less. Skim these quickly and put them in order, with the best paper on top. Go through the other piles in the same way until you have the whole set rank-ordered, best on top.

You can now go through the whole set and put letter grades on each paper.

Take a few notes on common problems and select one or two of the best papers to read to the class. When you return the papers to students, explain how you arrived at grades, mention the problems you noticed with the papers that weren't so effectively done, and read the samples so they can see how they might revise or rewrite their own papers.

This procedure can be modified in a variety of ways. For example, you can use four or six numbers instead of letter grades and rate each paper as you read it the second time. You can decide in advance what qualities are necessary in a paper for each grade or number, make a list, share it with students before they write their papers, and use it as a guide when you score the papers. Students can be taught to score each other's papers using such a scoring guide and will learn a great deal about how to improve their own work as they participate in the scoring process. (You can check over the papers later to make sure the ratings are fair or ask students to let you know if they want their paper reviewed again by you.)

Point System Evaluation

Make up a sheet which lists all the standards by which you will evaluate a student paper and assign each category a certain number of points. For example, organization might be worth 25 points; development, 50 points; and so on. Go over the sheet with students before they begin working on their papers and require that they hand it in with the final copy. As you read each paper, mark the number of points earned in each category, total them, and assign a letter grade according to the total points earned.

You can make this an additional opportunity for student learning by putting two sets of spaces for points on the evaluation sheet. Ask students to read a classmate's paper and rate it before turning in the paper and the rating sheet to you. When you return the papers, talk about the scoring as well as the papers themselves.

Highlighting

Instead of writing lengthy comments on student papers, highlight the problem area and tell students to bring their papers to you if they can't see how to improve the highlighted portions of their papers. (This method is a good way of marking mechanical errors, too. Have students work in pairs to figure out what the errors are and to assist each other in correcting them.)

As you teach, you'll think of new ideas to try. Be adventurous. If some method doesn't work well the first time, refine it and try it again. If something turns out to be a total disaster, remember that you aren't obligated to continue with it. Don't be afraid to tell students when you're trying something for the first time or that you made a mistake when something doesn't work out well. If they don't like a method you're using, ask them what they would suggest instead. Be brave and try some of their ideas, too. I've benefitted many times from suggestions my students have made.

CHAPTER SIX

MAKING THINGS EASIER FOR YOU AND YOUR SUBSTITUTE

As Mrs. Whitcomb surveys the chaos on her desk and listens to the students, she wonders if missing school to attend the conference was worth it. "We couldn't correct our homework papers yesterday because the sub couldn't find the answer key." "You should have seen what Jeffrey and Daniel did!" "He told us to read the next chapter, but I didn't have my book and he wouldn't let me borrow one so I haven't read it yet." "Mrs. Whitcomb, do subs get paid if all they do is yell and read the paper?"

IF YOU'VE HAD to cover a colleague's class and found yourself frustrated by a roomful of students who were difficult to manage and whose names you didn't know, then you have some idea what substitute teachers have to cope with most of the time. Day-to-day substituting is a tough way to earn a few dollars. Their job is often made even more difficult than it has to be when teachers fail to provide them with the basic tools they need for survival, such as seating charts and lesson plans.

Some substitute teachers are more capable and serious about their jobs than others, but you can increase the likelihood that some learning will take place in your classes when you are absent, no matter who fills in for you. You may have no control over the substitute who's hired, but you can influence your students.

STUDENTS CAN HELP

At the beginning of the year when you're discussing classroom behavior with your classes, take some time to talk about what they should do when guests come to the class. Anyone who comes in the classroom but is not a regular member of the class should be considered as a guest—a substitute teacher, the principal, another teacher, the student aide who delivers messages from the office, or a parent—and the students should put on their "company manners." Just as their parents expect them to behave better than normal when the family has company, you expect that they will be more helpful and more respectful when guests come to the class. Disruptive behavior and bad manners on these occasions are more serious offenses than they would be when you and the students are alone in the classroom. If you get bad reports on any of them from a substitute, you will take appropriate action when you return (perhaps an immediate phone call to a parent) and will not be very sympathetic to any explanation they try to offer after the fact. Most students will get the message. All you have to do is remind them periodically of your expectations and follow up as promised if a student doesn't cooperate.

If you have established routines in your classes, turned over some of the tasks to students, and given them calendar assignment sheets, they should be able to carry on in your absence without much help from the substitute. When I taught seventh grade social studies, I didn't spend much time in front of the class after the year got underway. A class president called the class to order, asked the class secretary to read the log from the previous day, and, after directing students to begin whatever activity was listed on their assignment sheet, checked to see that students had completed their homework. The students were so used to working on projects in small groups, presenting information to the rest of the class orally, and leading class discussions that I could have been absent for up to two weeks without much of a problem. A substitute was really needed only to satisfy legal requirements and sign passes.

Even though you may not want to relinquish as much control as I did, your students can be made more responsible for running the class when a substitute is there. The key is to prepare them in advance so they'll be ready when they need to be.

WHAT TO INCLUDE IN THE SUBSTITUTE SURVIVAL KIT

At the beginning of the year set up a folder which contains all the information a substitute will need to take over your classes and put it in a convenient place where someone else can easily find it should the need arise. The kit should contain information about where the sub can find a summary of school and class routines and procedures, copies of seating charts for all your classes, textbooks, supplies, forms, and emergency lesson plans (activities which can be completed in one period that may be substituted for your regular plans in case students are working on something a sub can't easily handle). If the school office doesn't provide the sub with a copy of the student handbook, include a copy in your folder with the relevant sections marked for easy reference. You might also include a copy of the teacher's handbook, if it's not too bulky, or photocopy the pages which may help the substitute.

Another option is writing a letter to the sub explaining how you have set up your class, what the basic rules and procedures are, the names of other teachers and students in each class the sub can call on for assistance, and what to do if there are problems. Pretend you're talking to the sub as you write. Make the letter friendly and informative. Imagine the questions a sub might have and answer them in your letter. It may help to think of what you'd like to know if you were going to take over the classes of someone you didn't know in an unfamiliar school. Writing this letter will help you clarify your own role as well as that of the sub. The easier you can make the substitute's job, the more your students will learn while you're away and the fewer problems you'll have to face when you return.

Dear Substitute Teacher,

Thank you for coming in to take over my classes today. All the books and materials you'll need are on my desk. Each class has a separate folder (in the standing desk file) in which you'll find a seating chart (Mark absences right on the chart), lesson plans, and papers to return to students. Please put any papers you collect and the list of students who did not have their homework done in the appropriate folder at the end of each class.

The names of students in each class who are in charge of opening the class, checking homework papers, reading the class log, and loaning materials, etc. are noted on the seating chart. Since the students know what they are to do at the beginning of the class, you'll have a little time each period to catch your breath and look over the day's lesson.

My sub folder contains my class schedule; information about school and class rules, homeroom and study hall procedures, and what you should do if there are any problems; and a couple of emergency activities to use in case something happens and you can't follow the regular lesson plan. The forms and passes you'll need are in the top right desk drawer. Call on Mary Ann Smalley who teaches next door if you need to. She'll be happy to help you out.

Would you please take a few minutes at the end of the day to fill out the sub report for me? (You'll find a copy in the sub folder.)

I hope that everything goes smoothly and you enjoy your day here. Thanks for your help.

Sincerely,

Anne Wescott Dodd

Figure 15. An example of a letter to the substitute teacher.

If you don't want to write a long letter, consider the shorter one shown here which lets the sub know where to find the other information.

Information the Sub Needs

- Your course schedule with times and room numbers
- Seating charts for homeroom, all classes and study halls
- Homeroom tasks
- Attendance procedures for homeroom, classes, and study halls
- Guidelines for issuing passes to locker, restroom, library, etc.
- Locations of books, resources, supplies, and forms/passes
- Routine class procedures, such as reading of class log, checking homework, collecting papers, etc.
- Special arrangements for information about individual students, if necessary
- What you'd like sub to do about students with whom they have problems
- What sub should do with papers they collect
- What teachers and students the sub can call on for assistance
- Where and when the sub can eat lunch (and location of nearest restroom, teacher's room, ditto machine, etc. You'd be amazed how many times substitutes have to figure these things out for themselves!)
- What you'd like the sub to leave for you at the end of the day

To be forewarned is to be forearmed; the more information you give the sub, the harder it will be for students to take advantage of the situation. Despite the fact that you prepare them in advance, some students, figuring that the sub won't know what's going on, will try to manipulate the sub into letting them do things they wouldn't normally be allowed to do. Make up a form on which the sub can note what was covered in each class and the names of students who were helpful, as well as those who were uncooperative.

EMERGENCY LESSON PLANS FOR SUBS

If your absence from school is planned in advance (to attend a conference, for example), you may be able to request that someone you know can sub for you. In this case, you may be able to have students continue on their regular assignments without interruption. You may wish to give students an extra day before turning in a major project or

SUBSTITUTE TEACHER REPORT

Date ______________________

Please note briefly what you did each period and how things went. I'd also like the names of students who were especially helpful to you as well as those who were uncooperative.

Period 1

Period 2

Period 3

Period 4

Period 5

Period 6

Period 7

What do I need to follow up on?

What else could I have done that would have made things easier for you today?

Would you be willing to come in for me again? Why or why not?

General Comments

Signed ____________________________, Substitute Teacher

Thank you for taking the time to fill this form out.

Figure 16. An example of a Substitute Teacher Report form.

paper, however, to avoid having some tell you when you fail to find their papers in the pile that they handed them in to the sub. Sometimes, however, either because the sub is not knowledgeable in your subject area (few subs can handle the content in a physics or calculus class) or because students are working on a specific assignment that you want to supervise personally from start to finish, you may want to forego the regular plans altogether. No matter what your subject area, you can develop some one-day activities which students can complete in one period and still learn something.

To make things easy on yourself and on the sub, develop emergency or optional lesson plans which won't require any advance preparation on the part of the sub, won't create commotion and confusion in the classroom, and won't leave you with a pile of papers to correct when you come back. That doesn't mean that the students shouldn't have anything to write down and turn in, but the assignment should be something which can be corrected in class or checked over by the sub so that the most you have to do the next day is enter a grade or check in your rank book.

Two or three such activities will probably be enough for the folder. After one has been used, replace it with a new one. (You may find that you'll want to use one of these activities yourself if following your regular lesson plans seems pointless because two-thirds of your class has gone on a field trip or has been excused from class to decorate the gym for the prom.) Because the sub may be called to come in at the last minute and will not have time to run off a ditto before class, make enough copies of handouts and collect any materials necessary for these activities and put them in the sub folder. (If the materials are too bulky to fit there, then just put one copy in the folder with a note indicating where the sub can find the rest.)

One-Period Activities

Some of the ideas listed below fit some subject areas better than others but can be adapted to work in a particular subject. Others are simply activities which develop critical or creative thinking—useful skills for students to develop no matter what subjects they are taking.

- A story or essay for students to read silently or for the teacher to read aloud with questions for follow-up discussion or writing
- Writing a letter to the editor of the school or local newspaper on an issue of concern to students

- Writing an editorial on a current or historical issue
- Trivia quiz adapted to particular subject (can be conducted like a spelling bee or students can write answers individually)
- Creating a new product and writing an ad for it
- Brainstorming contest— possible uses for a brick, toothpick, etc. (Can be done in small groups or individually)
- Making words from words—listing all the words that can be made, for example, from the letters which make up the name of the course
- Writing a letter of application for a part-time job
- Writing a poem, story, play, or children's book using terms or topic currently being studied
- Drawing a simple doodle or design on a paper and then writing directions for another student to follow to draw the same doodle or design without seeing the original one until after they've done their own
- Logic puzzles or mysteries to solve
- Writing a contest entry in 25 words or less—why study whatever the subject of the class is
- Inventing new words or a simple language
- Personification riddles: pretend to be an inanimate object, math or chemistry formula, historical figure, or literary character and write "I am . . . " followed by enough clues for other students to guess "Who am I?"
- Writing a diary entry of a fictional or historical character
- Writing a fifty-word summary of the last chapter students read in the textbook. Decide whose summary best covers the important points in the chapter
- Making up a crossword puzzle using names and terms from the subject area or topic currently being studied
- Writing questions to ask a famous person, historical figure, author, or literary character if students had the chance to meet him/her
- Creating a country (map for, description of government, and so on)
- Writing math problems and giving them to other students to solve
- Taking a paragraph or part of a chapter from the textbook and writing it so a student in a lower grade (third, fifth, etc.) could understand it
- Scavenger hunt for information in textbook, another book, or dictionary
- What would you do if . . . situations to write about or discuss
- Hunting for errors in the newspaper or on a handout
- Writing a news story or classified ad
- Analyzing advertising in a newspaper or magazine

- Spelling, math, or vocabulary bee
- Guessing what book, story, article, or TV program is about after hearing only the title
- Writing an original myth
- Writing copy for a dust jacket for textbook or other book
- Having students take notes in their own words on a photocopied entry from an encyclopedia and discussing whose notes best summarize the original material
- Handout to proofread or revise

After reading through the list above, you can probably think of other activities which would work with your classes. Your students will be more likely to cooperate with a substitute teacher if you plan interesting, enjoyable activities for them to do while you're away. Both the sub and your students may benefit from a break in the regular routine.

The more you help your substitute, the more you help yourself. If you plan well and prepare the students beforehand, it won't matter much who gets called to fill in for you and you'll have less work to do when you return.

CHAPTER SEVEN

WINNING SUPPORT FROM STUDENTS, PARENTS, AND SUPERVISORS

The principal stops Mr. Williams in the hall on the way to homeroom. "We've got a problem, Rich. Mr. Desjardins just gave me a earful. He doesn't understand how you can fail Johnny for not doing a project when the poor kid was sick. Frankly, I don't either. In any case, he and his wife will be in my office at 1:30 to meet with us. I'll get someone to cover your class. Don't be late. They've already threatened to go to the superintendent and the school board if you don't give the kid a fair shake."

TEACHING is a people-oriented profession. Anyone who has taught even for a short time realizes that it takes more than a knowledge of the subject to be successful in the classroom. Experts in any field will have a tough time trying to teach anyone if their people skills are weak. In fact, continuing conflicts with students, administrators, or parents are the reason some teachers get fired or leave the profession. Effective teachers have learned how to get along with the other people with whom they work—administrators, colleagues, secretaries, custodians, and, most important, students and their parents.

Both parents and students, like teachers themselves, want to feel valued and appreciated. While there's no way to guarantee that you'll be successful in making every student or parent feel that way, there are some things you can do to help students feel better about themselves and get parents to work with you rather than against you.

MOTIVATING STUDENTS

Perhaps the factor that most influences how successful students are at school is the image they have of themselves. That image has been developed to a large extent by their past experiences. Students who have relatively stable home lives, supportive parents, friends with whom they can share good times and disappointments, and past records of success both in and out of school will probably continue to do well with a little support and encouragement. They see themselves as having some control over their own lives, and they will be less likely to give up when things aren't going well. Other students are not so lucky. Because of chaotic home lives with alcoholic or abusive adults, undiagnosed learning disabilities, emotional problems, or the lack of support from adults or peers, some students see themselves as unlovable and incapable. They won't do well in school unless someone helps them to raise the level of their self-esteem. When teachers reinforce the image they have of themselves as failures, they cause problems in the classroom ranging from a refusal to do assignments, which is annoying but doesn't really affect other students, to hostile or antisocial behavior which can disrupt the whole class. You can motivate these students (and the others as well) by creating an atmosphere in your classroom which helps students develop and maintain positive self-concepts.

Don't pay much attention to what other teachers say about students in the teachers' room. You can often succeed with a student when others have failed. A feisty seventh grade girl transferred to my class after the first ranking period because her previous teacher could not deal with her rude and defiant behavior. She bounced into my room that first day and challenged me by announcing to the whole class that she was there because she had given her previous teacher a hard time. Fortunately, the other students were working on a writing assignment at the time and I was able to take her aside for a private conversation.

I first asked her to tell me what the problems had been in the other class. She was dying to tell me anyway, and I figured she might inadvertently provide me with information I could use to make sure she didn't cause the same problems in my class. It was clear from what she said that she loved to challenge authority and would go to almost any lengths to get attention from the teacher and her classmates. Naturally, she didn't care whether or not that attention was positive. As she talked, I made two mental notes: (1) to avoid a confrontation which she would turn into a power struggle and (2) to find ways she could get the attention she craved by helping rather than hindering the class. To make a long story short, I did both.

I welcomed her to the class, explained in a very neutral tone how the class was set up and what my expectations were, and invited her to let me know either orally or in her journal (one of the required class assignments) whenever she had any concerns about the way things were going or how I was treating her. This approach immediately put her off balance, since she couldn't use me as an object in her "get-the-teacher" game. Because she was so full of energy and ideas, the other students saw her as a leader and she got plenty of opportunities in class to satisfy her need for attention by chairing small group sessions and serving as the spokesperson for other students. I recognized and further reinforced her contributions and cooperation in class through comments on her journal entries. At the end of the year she presented me with a carefully wrapped package. She said she had earned the money for the bottle of cologne by ironing clothes for many hours.

Of course, no teacher can reach every student, but there are ways to increase the number you do reach. These successes, not the salaries they earn, are the real rewards for teachers.

Treat Students as People

The golden rule, "Do unto others as you would have them do unto you," works as well with students as it does with adults. That means avoiding sarcasm, put-downs, power struggles, threats, anger, and hostility. Even when you are tired or frustrated, keep your tone of voice neutral and calm. If a student displays anger, hostility, or frustration, don't respond in kind and make the situation worse. The student is probably not attacking you personally but responding to a situation in the only way he knows how. You can show the student that it's often a good idea to stay calm when someone else is upset, that problems are solved by discussion, compromise, and considering alternatives.

In thinking about your relationships with students, consider how you'd like to be treated by your department head or principal. Your students need the same kind of support and encouragement from you that you as a teacher would like from the people who have power over you. Remember, too, that people respond better to requests than they do to orders, and most will accept (even if they do not like) the idea of a change in procedure or some extra work if they understand why it is needed.

Show Students You Care About Them as Individuals

Take a personal interest in them by asking questions about their hobbies and out-of-school activities and complimenting them for their thoughtfulness or effort. Give them some choices about what they will study and how. Invite them to use free writings to comment on how the class is going, suggest changes, or let you know when they have problems with an assignment or deadline. Encourage them to share their ideas and experiences in class discussions. Even though you're not trained as a guidance counselor, take a few minutes to listen and talk with students who come to you with personal difficulties. You can't begin to solve the complicated problems some students face outside of school, but you can suggest people and places where they can get help.

Provide Multiple Opportunities for Success

Schedule regular after-school or study hall help sessions for those students who get behind or are having difficulty with the subject. Allow students to redo written assignments and retake tests for extra credit. Include enough variety in your assignments and teaching methods so that students who do poorly one time can succeed another time and sometimes can work cooperatively with another student(s) instead of struggling by themselves. Rather than requiring all students to do exactly the same assignment, list several options from which they may choose, whenever possible. Base part of the quarter grade on how much students choose to do so that they have some control over how much work they have and what grade they will get. Involve students in the process of determining their final grades.

Recognize and Reward Student Efforts and Accomplishments

Display and publish student work on the bulletin board and around the room; in class magazines, school newspaper or literary magazine, and publications outside the school; at open houses, art shows and science fairs. Encourage students to share what they've done in class with friends and parents. Praise students when they've done something well, for example: turning a paper in on time when they're usually late, scoring a goal in a soccer game, or performing in the drama club production. Write complimentary notes on student papers or, better yet, put the message on a postcard or in a letter and mail it home.

At the middle school where I was principal, we had blue (the school color) postcards printed at the top: "A Message from Freeport Middle School." Teachers used these to send good news home, and they weren't reserved just for great accomplishments. A student with a poor record for doing homework might get a postcard which said, "You've done your homework everyday this week! I'm pleased, and you should be proud of your efforts. Keep up the good work."

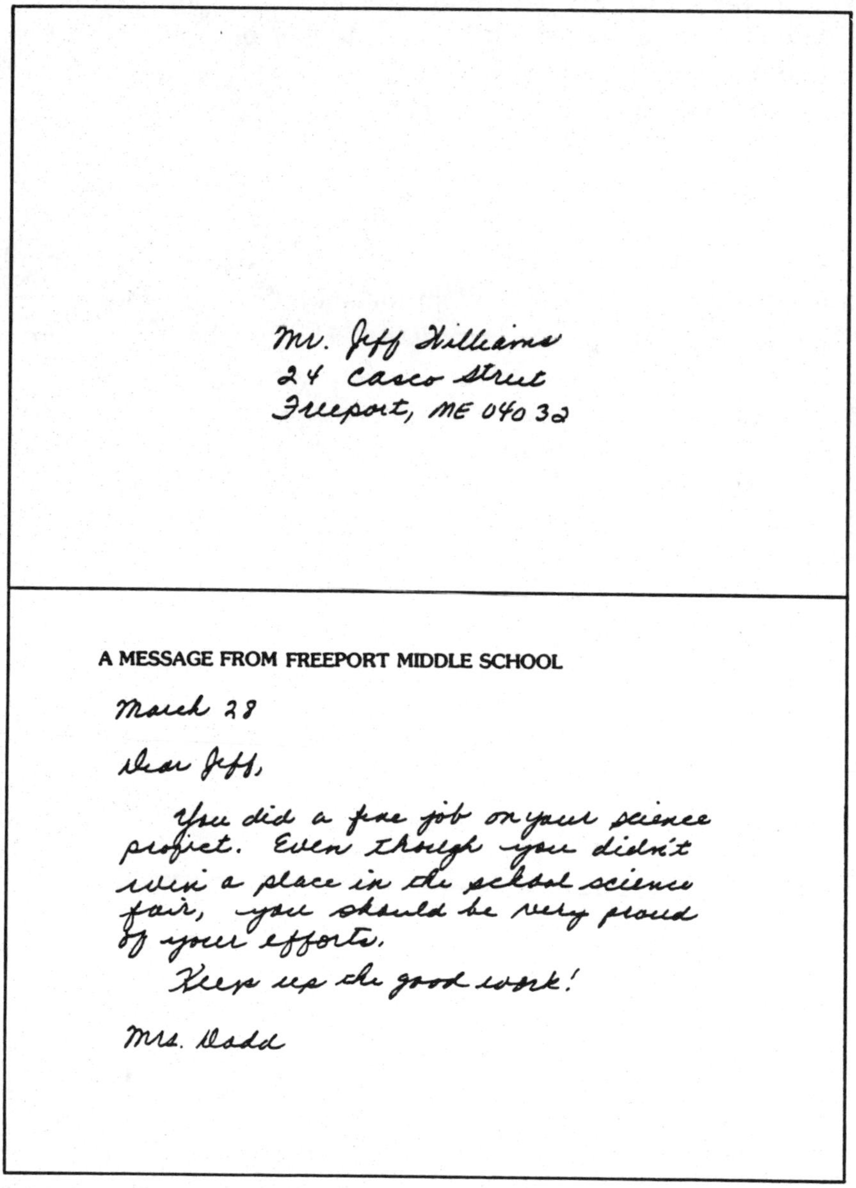

Mr. Jeff Williams
24 Casco Street
Freeport, ME 04032

A MESSAGE FROM FREEPORT MIDDLE SCHOOL

March 28

Dear Jeff,

You did a fine job on your science project. Even though you didn't win a place in the school science fair, you should be very proud of your efforts.

Keep up the good work!

Mrs. Dodd

Figure 17. An example of a postcard message. Teachers can encourage students and help build their self-esteem by writing personal notes and mailing them home.

Since most students rarely receive mail, you can imagine how good they felt when they found such a postcard waiting for them after a day at school. And not only do the parents feel good about their child's accomplishment, but they also have nothing but praise for the teacher who takes the time to write and mail the note. This is one way teachers can get a lot of mileage from a few minutes' effort.

Knowing that most students have a number of relatives and friends who might be interested in what they do, I keep a pair of scissors handy when I read the local paper and cut out photos or articles which mention my students to give to them. A couple of minutes here and there and a little thoughtfulness can go a long way to let students know that you care. You'll find that even the football star who is a marginal English or math student at best will begin to put a lot more effort into your subject when he sees that you notice how important he is to the football team.

The more you can do to help students feel good about themselves, the more they can do for themselves. The students who see themselves as hopeless failures won't become champions overnight, but you can help them achieve some small successes in your class on which they can build. The old cliché is still very true: nothing succeeds like success. All it takes for these students to begin the process is a caring teacher who helps them take the first step.

INVITING PARENTS TO GET INVOLVED

Research shows that students whose parents become involved with the school receive better scores on achievement tests and generally meet with more success in school than those who don't. For a variety of reasons, parents are more likely to be in closer contact with the school when their children are in elementary grades than later on. Because teachers in the early grades have the same students all day long and often depend on parent volunteers to help with school activities and field trips, they get to know students and their parents better than high school teachers. Parents, too, are more likely to participate in PTA and attend school performances when their children are young.

Older children often discourage their parents from getting involved, and some parents whose own school experiences were negative are happy to stay away. If the schools contact parents only when there's a problem, everyone loses. And it does no good when the parent learns about the situation after it's too late to influence the outcome. You can make your own job easier by letting parents know what's going on in your classroom, what you expect from students in terms of academic work and behavior, and what they can do at home to help the child as well. All parents want their children to succeed, and this is true even of parents whose own personal problems are the source of many of the difficulties their children have in school.

Many of these parents were themselves victims of hostile, uncaring teachers and assume that their children are experiencing the same kind of treatment. They fear the school and get defensive, often before they even find out why a teacher is contacting them. You have to break this cycle by changing the image they have of teachers and schools so that they can communicate a more positive attitude to their children. Show them that you respect them as parents and that you care about their child. If there is a problem, let them know about it when it's still small enough so that you can work with them and the child to solve it. Invite them to get involved and make that contact a positive experience. If your approach is, "I've got a problem and I need your help," the parent won't feel put down or under attack. Of course, communicating with parents *before* there's a problem is an even better way to win their support.

What You Can Do to Inform and Involve Parents

(1) Write a letter at the beginning of the year explaining what your course covers; the homework, grading, and makeup policies; what special activities are planned; when you're available to give students extra help; and what they can do at home, such as providing a time and place for doing homework, checking to see that homework is done, encouraging pleasure reading, and so on. You can give parents this information at an open house, but since many won't attend and those who do may not remember specifics, writing a letter is still a good idea.

(2) Send follow-up letters throughout the year to let parents know about special activities and projects and specific details when students begin a new unit of study.

(3) Provide parents with a copy of your calendar assignment sheet when students get behind in their work or will be out of school for a few days. Many parents will take the time and effort to make sure students do the assigned work, but they usually don't know what the child is supposed to do. If they know what is due and when, they can make the child show them the completed assignment instead of hearing, "We didn't

have any homework tonight." And, remember, parents have more ways to encourage compliance than teachers do! Take advantage of that fact and make your own job less difficult by giving them enough information to take over some of the responsibility.

(4) Have students write a class newsletter to let parents (and the principal) know what's happening in your class. The newsletter, which doesn't have to be fancy, also gives the students a chance to develop their writing skills and get public recognition for their efforts. It's also good PR for you.

(5) When students aren't doing well academically, let the parents know right away by clipping a short note to a poorly done assignment or failed test for students to take home for a parent's signature. But make a copy of the paper in question if you want to save it. I once wanted to keep an ancient history test with such creative responses as, "Rosetta Stone was a queen in ancient Egypt." When the student's mother read the test, she was so upset with her daughter's lack of effort, she wrote me a two-page letter instead of simply signing the test and returning it as I had requested. My effort paid off though: the girl got nothing less than A's and B's for the rest of the year.

(6) Let parents know early on when a student is having difficulty so that they still have time to do something about the situation before the end of the quarter in the case of missing assignments or before the student faces disciplinary action by the principal or vice-principal in the class of inappropriate classroom behavior. Parents can get very angry (and rightfully so) when things have been allowed to escalate out of control before they hear anything about it. Consider, too, how you would feel as a parent if the first call you get about your child's constant disruptive behavior in class came from the principal instead of the teacher.

(7) If your school schedules a schoolwide open house only once or twice a year, consider having students help plan some additional ones in your own classroom where they can display their work, perform skits or hold debates, and tell their parents what they're learning.

(8) Find ways you can use parents as volunteers in your classroom and invite them to participate. Parents who work may be able to help out by doing jobs in the evening if they can't come to school during class time. Parents can be of help in the following ways:

- Typing student work for class publications
- Providing transportation or accompanying students on field trips, to math meets, young writers' conferences, etc.

- Tutoring or working with small groups
- Speaking to the class about how their work, hobbies, or travel relate to what is being studied
- Substitute teaching when you are out (Many states do not require that substitute teachers be college graduates, and there's no better way for parents to find out how complex and demanding your job is than to step into your shoes for a day or two. They can also get new insights about their own children and children in general and often have fewer discipline problems than other subs because they know many of the children.)
- Serving as judges in classroom and school competitions
- Donating money or materials or helping raise funds for special class projects

Brainstorm other ways parents might become more directly involved with your class and assist you in the difficult job you do. Everyone—the parent, you, and the students—can benefit. It goes without saying that you should always remember to thank parents when they do help out. Make this an opportunity to teach students as well by having them write the thank-you notes and suggest other ways the class can recognize parent contributions.

AVOIDING CONTROVERSY AND CONFRONTATIONS

Controversies over issues, such as censorship, or policies, such as discipline, not only sap teachers' energy and demoralize them but, once these issues are magnified by the media, they can also cause people in the community to vote against school budgets and bond referendums. Individual teachers can often prevent situations from happening in the first place by anticipating the consequences of their action or lack thereof. All you have to do is raise your level of awareness about the possibility of a problem to take the right steps to prevent it.

When you select materials for your course, for example, consider the community in which you are teaching. If you plan to have students read a novel which may offend the sensibilities of some groups in the community, tell students at the outset that they have the option of substituting another book if they object or think their parents might object to their reading the book in question. (To determine which books might fall into this category, check one of the lists of the most censored books which are available from organizations, such as the National Council of Teachers of English.) Most parents are concerned primarily with the books their own children, not someone else's, are reading. By providing an option in the beginning, you're letting parents know that you realize not everyone shares the same values and you respect the rights of parents to make decisions regarding their own children.

High school students may not share their parents' views and are smart enough to know that what their parents don't know won't hurt them. When I described several books from which students could choose one to read for a unit I developed on schools, I explained that one book about an alternative school for tough, street-wise kids contained a great deal of language that many people would consider offensive and cautioned students not to choose this particular title if they felt their parents would object. You can guess what happened. I didn't have enough copies for everyone who wanted to read that book, and some students were unhappy that they had to choose another one. There were no repercussions, however, because the students who knew their parents might not approve never let their parents see the book. Another time a student, knowing that his parents wouldn't want him to read *The Catcher in the Rye* because they belonged to a very conservative fundamentalist church, read the whole novel in his study halls at school.

High school students (and younger children as well) are also smart enough to know how to cause trouble for a teacher when they want to. Raising questions about books or assignments is one way students can get revenge when they feel resentful or hostile towards a teacher. Given a book or an assignment that goes against the family's religious or personal values, all the student has to say to his parents is, "Just look what this teacher is making us read (do)!" Perhaps it's a young adult novel or a health text which mentions premarital sex or homosexuality, a values clarification exercise (who's allowed to stay on the life raft), or journal writing. Once the student calls the parents' attention to it, they'll do the rest and, taken by surprise, you'll find yourself on the defensive.

This kind of situation illustrates the importance of maintaining positive relationships with students. The only way to prevent a student's working against you in this way is to stay in touch with what students are thinking. Encourage them to come to see you when they feel you've treated them unfairly. And, because resentment and hostility develop over time, don't ignore a student's anger or hurt feelings, thinking they'll go away. They might; they might not. Resolve problems, big or small, as soon as they occur to prevent them from escalating and becoming unmanageable later. One way to make sure students aren't quietly raging inside is to give everyone several opportunities to recoup earlier losses and start fresh again.

Finally, students know how to manipulate a situation to their advantage, and they can easily get their parents to side with them against you if they tell their side of the story first. Although you may not like the idea of calling parents, consider what can happen when you don't.

Suppose you have spoken to Johnny several times about his long overdue project which represents a hefty portion of his quarter grade. You finally tell him on Friday that if he doesn't hand in the project on Monday, he will fail for the quarter. You feel you are being very generous. Johnny did miss a week of school early in the quarter due to illness, but he refused several offers from you to help him with the project after school. Three weeks ago he requested, and you agreed, to extend his deadline two extra weeks which meant that he should have turned the project in last Monday. Despite all these efforts, however, you didn't contact his parents about the missing work. There's the mistake.

Johnny wants to go skiing with his friend's family this weekend, so he goes home and tells his parents that he's going to fail your class if the project isn't finished, but he doesn't stop there. He goes on to tell them how unfair you are to flunk him for being sick and missing school. Of course, Johnny is presenting his parents with a very distorted version of the facts, but they don't know that. Johnny's been looking forward to the ski weekend for a long time and they don't want him to be disappointed. They're angry that a teacher would threaten a student with flunking the whole quarter when the poor child had a good reason for not having the project done.

Johnny's ploy works, but the parents don't call you; they go straight to the principal. So now you have to explain your side of the story to the principal as well (or maybe even the superintendent if you teach in a small town). If earlier you had made one phone call, you would probably already have the completed project in hand. Even calling the parents on Friday before Johnny had a chance to get home from school would have put Johnny on the spot instead of you. Now, probably nothing short of a conference with the parents, the principal, Johnny, and you will resolve the problem, and, no doubt, you'll be forced to extend Johnny's deadline again. One phone call and you could have saved yourself the wasted time and angry feelings.

Anytime you think there may be repercussions from a classroom incident or a continuing problem, such as the one described above, save yourself some hassle and put the responsibility where it belongs: on the student's shoulders. Talk to the parent before the student does, even if that means calling the parent at work while the student is still at school. If you do have to interrupt the parent on the job, apologize for calling, say that you need their help, and explain the situation calmly and clearly. Then Johnny will have all the explaining to do instead of you. By the way, if the incident is serious or the parents are not cooperative, let your principal know what's happened in case the parents decide to go to someone higher up. The information he has in advance both empowers him and protects you.

You can avoid most confrontation and controversy simply by treating people the way you'd like to be treated, by thinking ahead to prevent problems when you can, and by resolving the ones you can't avoid while they are small. Most important, because students learn best from the examples they see, you can teach them some valuable lessons about dealing with people and problems in their own lives without writing a lesson plan or giving a test.

GETTING SUPPORT FROM SUPERVISORS

Department heads, principals, and superintendents are people, too. They want to feel good about themselves and need support, encouragement, and positive feedback as much as you do. They don't often hear from anyone when things are going well, and they're the ones who have to deal with irate parents, complaining teachers, and demanding school board members. If you do your job well and try to make theirs easier, they'll be there when you need them. At some point you'll need a superior on your side for a recommendation for another position or admission into a graduate program, a special favor for personal or professional reasons, or backing when you have a problem with a student or parent. For your own protection, you need to get along even with administrators whom you consider incompetent. Consider the following suggestions for earning their respect and support.

(1) Meet deadlines and handle routine tasks efficiently. You may feel that filling out some form is a waste of time; perhaps they do, too, but they need information from you to write a report that *their* superior requires. If you fill the form out carelessly and fail to hand it in on time, you create extra work for them. If it will only take a few minutes, do it now and hand it in early. The principal will notice and remember.

(2) Follow district procedures and policies. For example, if you don't fill out the required form and turn it in on time, the principal may be forced to turn down your request for professional leave. If you can't attend a conference, it will be your own fault, not his. Part of his job is to see that policies and procedures are followed in the same way part of yours is making sure that students do likewise.

(3) Accept duty and committee assignments gracefully. You may not like the extra work, but it comes with the job. A tip: sometimes you can get on a committee that interests you or be assigned to a duty you prefer if you make a request in advance.

I was always at school very early in the morning and thought sitting in the hall for twenty minutes every day guarding the door to keep students from coming in before the bell (although I didn't think the policy was a good one) would be preferable to supervising a full-period study hall later in the day. I asked if I could have that duty and had no trouble getting it, since most of the other teachers didn't want to be obligated to get to school early everyday. The forty-five minutes I had free later was a godsend.

(4) Handle discipline problems yourself, referring only the most serious ones to the administrators. Like the boy who cried wolf, many teachers don't get help when they really need it because they routinely burden the vice-principal with little things they should have handled themselves. If you request assistance only when it's necessary, your requests will be taken seriously.

(5) Keep administrators informed and let them hear good news as well as bad. The more they know about what's happening in the school, the better they can do their jobs, whether it's solving a problem with an unhappy parent or letting community members know that exciting and interesting activities are going on in the classrooms.

(6) If you feel the urge to critize the way something is being handled, go directly to the administrator, who has the power to change things. Griping in the teachers' room serves no purpose except to make everyone feel more miserable. Maybe you can't change anything, but you'll never know unless you try.

I learned how to develop a master schedule for the school because I was unhappy about the way the English classes were scheduled for the second semester. The principal listened to my complaints and invited me to work with him on a revision of the schedule. The English classes got changed, and I learned that scheduling isn't as simple as it appears. I put the knowledge, which one usually can't get in college courses on administration, to good use several years later when I was hired as an assistant high school principal and had to develop a master schedule from scratch without the help of someone who had done it before.

(7) Try looking at things from an administrator's point of view. Ask yourself what you'd do about X if you were in charge. What you'll discover may surprise you. Often, the administrator is doing just what you would do.

(8) If you can think of ways to change procedures or policies which might make the school run more smoothly and improve morale, share those ideas with an administrator. Bogged down in the details of the job, the principal may not have thought of any other way to do things and may be very willing to give what you suggest a try.

(9) Don't blame administrators for enforcing provisions in the negotiated contract. Although principals usually have little to do with the negotiation process between the school board and the teachers' association, they have the responsibility, for example, not to allow teachers to take personal days for reasons not specified in the contract. If you don't like the way the contract is worded, don't attack the principal. Talk to the association representative about changing the wording the next time the contract is on the bargaining table.

I once taught in a school where the teachers voted to express their lack of confidence in the superintendent who had done nothing more nor less than follow the negotiated contract to the letter. Rather than wasting time and energy complaining about the superintendent for doing his job, these teachers would have been better off to study the wording of the present contract, resign themselves to playing the game by the present rules for now, and begin planning how to negotiate the changes in the rules as soon as the contract comes up for renewal. Understanding *how* people operate is the first step in figuring out how to go about getting what you want from them.

(10) Treat administrators as people. Compliment them once in a while. Thank them when they do something for you. Look for ways to stroke their egos and make them feel good about what they do. If the stress gets to you and you lose your cool and take it out on them, apologize. Your efforts will not go unnoticed, and you will get back what you give.

Winning friends and influencing people—students, parents, administrators, colleagues, relatives, and friends—really comes down to nothing more than being a caring, considerate person who is quick to notice and praise the good in others and overlook or at least downplay the bad. If you expect people to be friendly, honest, reliable, and well-intentioned, most of the time they will be. And when problems do arise, many times you can discover a solution just by looking at the situation from the other person's point of view.

CHAPTER EIGHT

SURVIVING AS A PERSON AND GROWING AS A PROFESSIONAL

Ginger, a first-year teacher, sits in the coffee shop with a college friend who's doing graduate work. "I knew the first year would be tough, but it's harder than I thought. I'm getting by, but there's so much I don't know. What I really miss is what I had as a student teacher—someone to talk things over with, help me figure out how to handle a problem with a student, suggest new things I can try. I never see the really good teachers—they're too busy—and the ones I do see in the teachers' room spend all their time complaining. Just listening to them gets me so down, I've stopped going in there. I never thought teaching would be so lonely."

HOW OFTEN have you heard burnout cited as the reason teachers leave the profession? If you've been teaching any length of time, you know how demanding and stressful the job can be, but you also know that many teachers don't burn out. Why not?

Unless they're looking for a way to earn more money, people who give up on teaching usually do so for one of three reasons. They don't have the right constitutional makeup for the job in the first place, they never get personally involved in the job, or, conversely, they get too involved. Even though you're still teaching, you may have thought about looking for a job outside of education yourself. Do you see any similarities between you and any of the three teachers described below?

After two years of teaching high school social studies, Barry decided to leave teaching for a job selling books for an educational publisher. Almost from the very first day Barry was frustrated with the students' lack of interest and motivation, his inability to determine his own schedule, and the demands administrators imposed on him. An impatient person, he got irritated every time students asked questions about an assignment he had just explained. He never considered the fact that his directions might have been confusing; he figured the students just didn't listen. He also disliked going through the same routine day after day, spending time after school discussing the same old problems in faculty and curriculum committee meetings, and, most of all, dealing with teenagers, who, as far as he could tell, were rude, lazy, and very selfish. Clearly, teaching was the wrong job for Barry.

Mary Ann, a junior high school math teacher, taught five years before she resigned to become a management trainee in private industry. Mary Ann liked her students well enough, but she never got to know them very well. She came to school each morning, presented the lesson, answered students' questions, collected their papers to correct later, supervised students at lunch, and attended required meetings and school activities. Although occasionally things didn't go as she had planned, she coped and had little to complain about. But after teaching from the same eighth grade math book for several years, she found the job rather boring and wanted to try something else. Because Mary Ann distanced herself from her students and her teaching, she never discovered the challenges and rewards that teaching can offer. Mary Ann burned out because she never got personally involved in what she was doing.

Unlike Barry, Karen, a high school English teacher, loved teaching when she began. In many ways she was sorry six years later when she decided to give it up to work for a public relations firm. Students begged to get into Karen's classes because of her reputation as an exciting and creative teacher. She let her students have some say in what they learned and how, invited guest speakers to come to her classes, and took students on field trips several times a year. Karen was involved with students outside of class as well. She advised the school drama club, the literary magazine, and the football cheerleaders, and she was always available to help students who wanted to submit their work to a writing contest or needed someone to talk to. Karen was also active professionally, serving as the secretary of the state English teachers' association, attending conferences, reading professional literature, and working on school district and state curriculum committees. Everyone agreed that, by any measure, Karen was an outstanding teacher. But in taking on so many responsibilities, Karen gave too much time and energy to her job and had none left for herself. She did the right things to avoid burnout, but she did them to excess. Karen was too involved in teaching.

If you like young people and have plenty of patience, tolerance, stamina, and a sense of humor, you're probably in the right job. To enjoy teaching, get involved in what you're doing. Keep up with new developments in your field, try new methods and techniques, and look for new ways to help students meet with more success. But set limits on how much time and energy you devote to the job. Spend some time with people whose jobs have no connection with education, travel, garden, or read for pleasure.

Some of you have other balls to juggle outside of school—young children, second jobs, or college classes—which require more of your time and energy. To stay psychologically healthy, you must set aside some time each day just for you. Just fifteen minutes a day—maybe a cup of coffee in the morning before everyone else gets up, an after-school jog or racquetball game, a long shower or hot bath at night—can make a difference.

MANAGING AND REDUCING STRESS

We hear so much about the negative effects of stress, we often forget that some stress is actually beneficial. A little stress adds to a bit of spice to daily life in much the same way seasoning flavors food. What you need to avoid is too much stress, the kind that wears you down, debilitating you psychologically and physically. In fact, people don't often realize that many physical ailments can be the result of too much stress.

You can handle greater levels of stress without any ill effects, however, if you feel that you do have some control over your own life, you see problems as challenges you can overcome, and you are committed to what you do.

Learn to identify those times when you're feeling overwhelmed and suffering from the effects of too much stress. If you catch yourself barking at a colleague or a student in response to a simple question, chances are you are under too much stress. Figure out what's causing it and see if there's something you can do to change the situation. If not, decide that you can at least control your words and actions to avoid causing stress for someone else. Several suggestions for managing and reducing stress appear below.

(1) If you feel like snapping at someone, count to five or ten before you speak.

(2) If the pressure has been building and you feel ready to explode, take a deep breath in, hold it to the count of five, and then slowly let it out. Repeat once or twice until you feel more relaxed.

(3) When you've been sitting at your desk or in a meeting for a long time, get up. Look out the window, do some stretching exercises, go for a walk, get some fresh air.

(4) When you've been working on a problem and can't get the solution or trying to write a report and can't find the right words, stop. Do something else and let your subconscious continue working while you read a book or wash the car. You'll often find when you go back to the task later, you can finish it without any difficulty.

(5) Set limits on how much time and how much effort you will devote to individual tasks. Don't try to do everything perfectly. You don't need to spend as much time, for example, going over homework papers as you would on tests. Decide which jobs are more important and spend the bulk of your time and effort on them.

(6) Get in the habit of skim reading when you can. When a new issue of a professional journal comes, look through the whole issue and mark the articles you want to read carefully later.

(7) If problems with a student or supervisor continue and what you've been doing isn't working, stop. Reassess the situation. Use brainstorming or clustering to come up with new strategies to try. It's truly amazing how many people continue to repeat the same behavior even after they realize they're getting nowhere. Sometimes they'd be better off to save their energy and do nothing.

(8) Give yourself the pleasure of feeling you've accomplished something by setting goals for the week, the month, and the year. Evaluate your progress at regular intervals and revise your list. Don't make the goals too difficult to achieve, however, or you'll be more discouraged later than you are now.

(9) Use your planning period wisely. Spend part of it grading papers so you don't have to carry them home, but take some time just to unwind.

(10) If you feel overloaded, make a list of everything you have to do and then organize the tasks in order of priority. See if there are any you can delegate to someone else or forego doing altogether. Schedule time to do the others and get to work. People who get behind see all the things they have to do as one big unmanageable burden. Looked at that way, they see no way they can do anything except worry. Worrying makes things worse because it increases the level of stress without reducing the burden.

(11) Break big jobs into smaller pieces, then tackle them one at a time. The old cliché, "Life is hard by the yard but a cinch by the inch" is really true.

(12) Don't be afraid to say no. You know what your limits are. If the principal asks you to attend a district meeting in place of a colleague who can't make it and you really don't have time, tell him you'd like to help out but you can't do so this time. Nothing increases your stress level faster than getting into something when you should have said no in the first place. Not only are you less likely to do a good job at whatever it is, but you'll also feel resentful and probably end up taking those negative feelings out on someone else.

(13) If for political or personal reasons you really can't say no or the obligation is part of your normal responsibilities, then do the required task and think about how what you're doing will help you. If you can find no redeeming value in a boring in-service presentation, you may be able to learn something by examining the reactions of other people in the audience or by analyzing the speaker's performance to determine why it isn't effective and how it could be improved. What you discover may keep you from making the same mistakes in your own classroom. In any case, by keeping your mind busy you can prevent stress from building up.

(14) Don't let waiting for someone who's late upset you. Carry a book or papers to grade to keep yourself from dwelling on your irritation. People-watching is another good way to occupy yourself and help the time pass more quickly.

(15) When a person or problem infuriates you to the point that you honestly feel you could murder someone, ventilate. Punch a pillow, go somewhere private to yell and swear, talk to a friend, or write out all your anger on a piece of paper. Don't try to keep such powerful negative feelings inside; you'll suffer both psychologically and physically by doing so.

(16) Choose the situations where you will stand your ground. Some principles and issues are more important than others. Reserve your time and energy for the ones that really count. If the vice-principal insists that a warning is enough for the student who skipped your class and you feel the student deserves a suspension, state your views. But if the vice-principal refuses to yield, ask yourself, "What difference will this make in five years?" Asking that question puts the situation in perspective and is a good check to see if what you want to make a matter of principle is really worth all the trouble and aggravation that will follow.

(17) Don't be afraid to compromise. Sometimes the only solution when two people are at loggerheads is for each of them to move towards the middle. And sometimes you should even consider giving in. The stress that's caused by both of you stubbornly refusing to give a little can be more damaging to you than swallowing your pride.

(18) An apology even when you weren't in the wrong can sometimes do more good than holding your ground. Consider a heated discussion with a parent who feels you've treated her child unfairly. If you've tried to explain the circumstances and the parent refuses to hear you, what will you gain if the parent leaves with hostile feeings? What will the student gain? Say, "I'm sorry. Perhaps you're right. Maybe I have been too hard on Jeremy. I'll do my best to make sure I treat him fairly from now on." Saying that doesn't mean that you were wrong before or that you have to do anything differently in the future, but by seeming to apologize, you may be able to win the parent's support and make your life easier in the future.

(19) Asking questions to find out why someone else doesn't agree with you is also a good move. Also, try to see the situation from the other point of view. You may then be able to see how you can change the person's mind, but even if you can't, you'll find it easier to accept his position. And it always helps to think how dull life would be if everyone agreed on everything.

(20) Finally, don't waste time dwelling on what can't be changed. If you can't do anything about a situation, accept it and deal with the limitations it imposes on you.

IMAGING: A USEFUL TECHNIQUE FOR YOU AND YOUR STUDENTS

Through imaging, or visualization, you can put your subconscious mind to work to help you do whatever it is you want to do, from completing a complex project to getting through a difficult social situation or job interview. All you have to do is create mental pictures of the way you want things to turn out.

Losers are losers because they see themselves as losers. Because they expect to fail, they unconsciously behave in ways that actually cause them to fail. On the other hand, because successful people expect to succeed, they unconsciously behave in ways that increase their chances for success. The expectations we set for ourselves are more powerful than those others set for us.

Here's how imaging can help you create positive expectations. Perhaps you feel awkward and uncomfortable about meeting new people, especially in social situations, and the principal has asked you to represent the school at a reception for state legislators and educators in a neighboring school district. You dread going because you're sure you won't be able to make small talk or you'll say the wrong thing. When you first find out you'll be going to the reception, take a few minutes several times everyday to picture yourself already there. Run a movie of the event in your mind. Picture yourself walking into the room, confident and purposeful. See yourself going up to people, smiling, shaking hands, and chatting. Watch them respond warmly to you. Imagine driving home, happy that you had a chance to meet and talk with so many interesting people. What you picture yourself doing, you and your subconscious will come to believe and work to make it happen.

The same principle also applies to understanding a difficult concept or giving a speech. Picture yourself successfully handling a task which applies that concept or speaking to a responsive audience. The technique can also be used to lose weight or to quit smoking. See yourself as already thin and trim or feeling comfortable without a cigarette in a place where you normally smoke.

To make imaging work, you must see clear pictures like photographs in your head and you must look at them often. Picturing something once won't be enough to convince you and your subconscious that you really mean business. And if you've lived for a long time with a different image of yourself, you'll have to work hard to erase that deep-seated negative image. When you begin visualizing yourself in a positive way, be careful not to let intermittent glimpses of the "old you" interfere with your progress.

If you have doubts about the effectiveness of this strategy, try it first on a simple goal, such as writing a long-overdue letter to a college friend or making a phone call you've put off. You'll find that imaging is a good way to get yourself to complete projects on which you've procrastinated.

Tell your students about imaging, too, and check the results. For example, before the next unit test, ask them to close their eyes and picture themselves sitting in class the next day when the exams are passed out. Ask them to watch themselves confidently answer every question because they understand the material and finish in time to check their answers. Point out that imaging won't substitute for studying for the exam, but it will help them do better because they won't be prevented from using what they do know by anticipating failure before they begin.

Imaging doesn't take much time and it can make a very positive difference for you and your students. Try it. What have you got to lose?

USING PERSONAL ACTIVITIES AND INTERESTS IN YOUR CLASSROOM

Even though there are some good reasons for separating your personal life from your teaching, what you do outside of school can often enrich and improve your teaching.

When you take courses, even those that are unrelated to your teaching such as a sailing or craft course, you're the student. Many people who teach adult ed enrichment courses aren't trained as teachers, so you may learn from them what not to do. On the other hand, even though they have never taken a methods course, they may have learned what works from long experience so you may instead discover a new approach you can adapt in your own classroom.

Notice how you feel when you can't get the hang of a new skill or idea right away. When my husband (who isn't good in math) complained about the difficulty he had understanding what was going on in the celestial navigation class that he took, he reminded me that some of my students must feel similarly overwhelmed and confused in my writing classes. If you have to take a course to get recertified and you find the class boring, remember that many of your students may feel the same way about the course you teach. An awareness of what it's like to be a student can help you become a better teacher.

Consider ways that courses you take can apply to your classroom even though at first glance it appears that there's no connection. At one point I thought I might like to become a guidance counselor, so I enrolled in an introductory counseling course. Even though the course focused on showing how a therapist would interact with clients in a counseling session, I discovered that these same techniques were very useful in my writing classes. Students began to open up and talk more freely about their own work when I used some counseling leads/responses, such as silence, restatement, clarification, and reflection in conferences and encouraged students to do likewise in small group sessions. Methods of closing a client interview (summarizing what was said, giving a specific assignment, setting a time for the next meeting, and mentioning what wasn't talked about) also helped to make conferences and small group sessions more productive.

Many teachers share their outside interests with their students. One science teacher who loves his field developed a merit-demerit system for getting students to work and behave appropriately in class. Students earned points which enabled them to spend one Saturday on a boat watching whales frolic and another at the Boston Museum of Science. An English teacher with an interest in local history organized an interdisciplinary unit for junior high students which got them out of the classroom to do an archeological dig at the site of what was once a nineteenth century farm.

Informal sharing can be effective, too. Let students know about books you've read or movies you've seen that they might enjoy, too. If your hobby is arts and crafts, use some of your own work to decorate your classroom. If you write for publication, tell students about the difficulties you encounter. If they know you can handle rejection slips from publishers, they won't feel so bad when some of their efforts are less than successful. Because you are a powerful role model for your students, they can learn a great deal just from seeing you as a person with a variety of interests outside of school as well as a teacher.

REFLECTIVE TEACHING AND CLASSROOM RESEARCH

After one teacher complained that he was fed up with teaching and wanted out, his colleague later told me, "That guy hasn't taught for twenty years. What he's done is teach the first year twenty times." Therein lies the problem. When teachers teach the same subject in the same way year after year, they lose interest in their work. Moreover, if they do nothing differently, then they also continue to face the same problems day after day. Teachers who engage in reflective teaching and classroom research not only find their work more stimulating and challenging, they also discover ways to solve many of the problems they encounter in the classroom.

The Reflective Teacher

If when you are doing unit plans on a topic you have taught before, you consider what didn't go well the last time you taught the unit and make changes which should make things go better this time, then you already are a reflective teacher. You can do an even better job if you also consider gathering information to improve your teaching in other ways.

Keep a Teaching Journal Throughout the Year

Get a spiral-bound notebook and keep it handy. Spend a few minutes a couple times a week writing down your thoughts about how things went in your classes. If several students were confused about an assignment or did it all wrong, note that fact and any ideas you now have about how you might have made your expectations clearer to them. The teaching journal is also a good place to record the ideas for new methods you pick up from reading professional journals or conversations with colleagues. A year from now when you're making plans to teach the same material again, you'll have detailed notes to jog your memory so that you don't make the same mistake twice or forget to include an interesting activity you heard about and wanted to try. If you don't write those good ideas down, you're apt to forget them. If you jot them down on little slips of paper, you may lose or misplace them. If you have the self-discipline to record them in your teaching journal on a regular basis, however, you'll have the information available where you can find and use it later.

Ask Students for Feedback

Have students do a free writing after you've tried a new activity or at the end of the unit. Ask them to tell you what they learned, what they liked and disliked about the lesson, and what you might do differently the next time. Much of what happens in the classroom happens inside people's heads, so you have no real way of knowing students' perceptions unless you ask them. You may find out that things went better (or worse) than you thought they did. Even if the students don't make specific suggestions for improvements, their comments may lead you to think of changes which wouldn't have occurred to you if you hadn't first read what they had to say.

You can also gather information from students in a more structured way by making up questionnaires. Even on these, however, make it a point to have some open-ended questions or a free writing response at the end so the students have an opportunity to comment on something which the questionnaire didn't mention specifically. What you didn't think to include may be more important than what you did.

Videotape Yourself Teaching

The best way to see how you really come across in front of the classroom is to watch yourself teaching. You may notice that you dominate class discussions more than you realize, that your explanation of an assignment was confusing, or that you have personal habits which you should work to change, such as repeating a pet word or phrase or talking too fast. Several of my student teachers, for example, unconsciously used *"okay"* excessively, both at the beginning and end of most of their sentences: "Okay, you'll have thirty minutes to work on the test. Then we'll exchange papers and correct them in class. Okay?" My own downfall is speaking so fast that students often have trouble following what I'm saying. Someone can tell you about such behavior, but you may not realize how distracting it really is until you see yourself in action on videotape.

Invite Another Teacher to Observe Your Teaching

One advantage of having another teacher observe you as you teach a class is that she can also notice what students are doing. The classroom environment is so complex that you can focus only on a very small piece of it while you're teaching, and your perceptions may not match what's actually happening. Although an outside observer can't see everything either, she can, for example, record what students you call on and how often. (You could also ask a student volunteer to be an observer and record information as clear-cut as this.) An observer might notice that Susie was busily finishing her math homework when you assumed she was taking notes on your Civil War lecture. What's more, another teacher in your subject area may also be able to suggest other approaches for you to consider.

If the school schedule makes it impossible for the teacher you'd like to have watch you teach to do so, let him watch a videotape of your class. Even though the camera won't be able to pick up as much of what's happening as an observer in the room could, your colleague may still be able to give you valuable feedback.

When you ask someone else to watch you teach, be sure to give him some background about the students and the lesson before he observes and, to make the most efficient use of his time, tell him what you'd like him to look for. He will probably notice other aspects of your teaching anyway, but knowing what you want to focus on will make his feedback much more useful to you.

Teacher as Researcher

Many teachers are unaware of much of the research which has been done on teaching and learning because the university professors who do the studies usually report their results only in obscure academic journals classroom teachers rarely read. This situation is changing, however, for two reasons. In making decisions about tenure and promotion, some colleges and universities now also consider publication in the journals teachers do read and public service, such as working with public school teachers, as well as more traditional research activities. At the same time, many elementary and secondary teachers have begun doing research in their own classrooms, sharing what they have learned with others, and earning professional recognition for their efforts.

If you've lost some of the enthusiasm you had for teaching when you first began, doing some informal research in your own classroom is perhaps one of the best ways to rekindle it. You don't have to study hundreds of students and analyze complex statistical data to do so. A teacher researcher is an observer, a questioner, and a learner. You may wish to test the results of someone else's research with your own students or you can ask your own questions and look for answers.

Are there recurring problems in the classroom you'd like to solve? Is there some skill or concept that students never seem to quite get? Do you want your students to participate more actively in class discussion? Would you like to see them get more excited about the subject you're teaching? Do you want them to take more responsibility for their own learning? Do you wonder if there's any relationship between the amount of time students spend on homework and their success in your class? Do you have questions about individual students: Why doesn't Judy like to write? Why is Stephen so reluctant to get involved in class discussions? Why won't Arthur ever complete an assignment?

By turning a problem into a question, you're setting the stage for an investigation which may take the form of case study if your concern is an individual student or may evolve into a new set of lesson plans if you want to try new methods in order to increase student participation in discussions, for example. Once you've decided what you want to change or learn more about, make a plan. Decide how you are going to approach the problem and what you need to do in what order. Plans will vary. Two examples appear below.

Why Judy Doesn't Like to Write: A Case Study

(1) Statement of current situation: Describe specifically what Judy has said and done (or not done, such as voluntary writing) to indicate a dislike for writing.

(2) Information to gather which may lead to an answer:

- Look for journal articles and books for information which may suggest reasons and thus help me decide what to look for in the files and questions to ask Judy and others.
- Read Judy's school file.
- Read through all the writing in her class folder.
- Talk with Judy.
- Interview Judy's parents.
- Talk with previous teachers and maybe guidance counselor.

(3) Conclusions: Write up summary of what I find out.

(4) Follow-up: Examine my conclusions and figure out ways I might change her attitude.

The follow-up might result in constructing another plan which would be similar in design to the one that follows.

Getting Students To Work More Effectively in Small Groups

(1) Statement of present problem: Students waste a lot of time before getting busy when they work in small groups. One or two students in a group usually do most of the work. The room is noisy. Some students continue to disrupt those who are working even after they've been spoken to.

(2) Information to gather:

- Survey present student attitudes about small group work (construct questionnaire).
- Read journal articles and books on small group process.
- Ask other teachers for suggestions.

(3) Formulate lesson plans based on strategies I discovered.

(4) Implement in classroom—observe students and take notes.

(5) Evaluate results:

- Survey students again or ask for free writing.
- Summarize my observation notes.

(6) Follow-up: Make plans for future classes— what to do the same; problems that still need to be addressed.

Even though you can tackle only one question or problem at a time, you can see how, over time, you will improve your effectiveness as a teacher, but you may not realize another advantage of doing classroom research. When you get involved in looking for solutions to classroom problems, you'll be so busy looking for answers and so interested in finding out how a new strategy will work that you won't take time to complain when things aren't going well. In fact, after successfully using the research approach to solve an instructional problem or to get an unmotivated student excited about learning, you may even begin to welcome the existence of new problems because they present a challenge, a new area to investigate.

The best teachers are lifelong learners, and, besides learning more about their own disciplines, they continue to learn more about teaching and learning. Look around your school. Which teachers are burned out? Which teachers are dead wood? If your school is like most other schools, the teachers who fit in these categories are the ones who have stopped learning and growing. Many of them are in as much of a rut outside of school as they are inside. The secret to staying interested and involved in teaching is looking for ways to do the job better. The search itself energizes.

RENEWAL THROUGH PROFESSIONAL INVOLVEMENT

Professional activities offer many benefits, among them: knowledge and skills to help you teach more effectively; personal recognition to increase your own feelings of self-esteem; support from colleagues—both near and far—to make the isolation that comes with the job easier to bear; and power to effect change not only in your own classroom but also in your school and beyond.

Your commitment can be as small in scope as serving on a local committee or attending a conference, or as large as accepting state or national office in the professional organization which represents your subject area. Choose the activities that most appeal to you and realize that once you do get involved, you may "get hooked." Then, you'll have to be careful to resist the tendency to say yes too quickly. Don't accept more responsibilities than you can handle.

In your own school and school district there are a number of committees which need teacher representatives. Some have more power or prestige than others. Instead of waiting to be assigned to a committee in which you have little interest, volunteer for one which allows you to do something for you. For example, if you think the in-service programs have been useless or poorly designed, don't waste time and energy complaining about them in the teachers' room; get on the committee which plans them and work for change. What is true for staff development is also true for other areas. If you have too many students in your classes or think the personal-leave policy for the district is too restrictive, join the teachers' association negotiating team and make sure those items are included in the next round of bargaining with the school board on the master contract.

Professional organizations, such as the National Council of Teachers of English, the National Science Teachers Association, or the National Council for the Social Studies, exist for teachers in every subject area. Most also have state organizations as well. Through the conferences they sponsor and the journals they publish, you can keep up with recent research in your field and get new ideas for teaching. Some of these organizations are also becoming more active politically in an effort to prevent state and national legislators from passing new laws which make teaching more difficult. But what you may appreciate the most are the professional meetings where you can meet and talk with teachers who teach in other communities or in other states.

If you teach in a small school where the other two people in your department are "retired on the job" and would only try something new if they got extra pay for doing so, you'll find the stimulation and encouragement you can get at a conference from talking with teachers who are excited about teaching will renew your spirits and keep you going when you're back home. Knowing that teachers elsewhere have the same problems you do somehow makes living with them easier, and sometimes others have found solutions which they will share. If you don't know anything about the organization which represents teachers in your subject, find out. You don't know what you're missing.

Professional involvement can also help you in your career. If you write and publish an article about what you have learned from your own classroom research, you may be hired by another school district to present a workshop for teachers there. Both items will look good on your résumé if you apply for a position in another district or for a promotion in your own. The three years I was in charge of the annual three-day conference for an English association taught me a great deal about planning, organizing, and working with people. I'm sure that having had that experience helped me get hired for my first administrative position (high school assistant principal) but, even more important, the skills I developed helped me succeed once I started on the job. And if you decide to leave education for a career in some other field at some point in the future, what you do outside the classroom added to your teaching experience will make you more employable.

These professional activities do take extra time. You may be thinking you've got all you can do to keep up with what you're doing now. Many teachers, however, would agree with the high school English teacher who told me recently, "I come to these Saturday meetings [of the executive board of the state English organization] several times a year, and I'm always exhausted when I leave the house. I think I'd rather stay in bed late than drive an hour to a meeting of teachers. But, you know, it's surprising. I leave less tired than when I came. After talking with the others here while we're stuffing folders or discussing ways to increase membership, I feel better about myself and the job I do." Because a great deal of social interaction comes with doing more professionally, people do feel refreshed even though they're doing more, not less. Try it and see.

Consider, too, the idea of joining with other kindred souls in your own school or district to learn and grow. Because such a group can meet personal as well as social and professional needs, you'll find that meeting with other teachers on a voluntary basis just once a month for coffee and conversation will energize you and lift your spirits. Talk about what you're doing in your own classes, learn about something new, or simply meet to discuss articles or books you've read.

If the district can provide some funds, you might consider inviting guest speakers. In one town teachers who wanted to learn more about teaching writing met after school for coffee once a month. They heard a short presentation—writing across the curriculum one month, journal writing the next—followed by refreshments and informal conversation with the consultant.

In another district a small group of elementary and middle school teachers along with the middle school principal formed their own writing/discussion group. They met two afternoons a month throughout the school year to talk about teaching writing and to share drafts and get advice on their own writing projects. (Several members later had their work published.) Because the teachers also discussed how they were teaching students to write, they learned from each other. One teacher who was having difficulty motivating the students in one of her classes got good results when she tried activities suggested by her colleagues.

Sometimes the group also got involved in spirited discussions about education in general, and, though they didn't come to any conclusions, everyone agreed the exchange of ideas was interesting and beneficial.

Figure 18. These middle-school teachers encouraged and supported each other by meeting informally after school to talk about their own writing and share ideas on teaching students to write. Photo courtesy of the Bath-Brunswick (Maine) *The Times Record.*

Getting together with other teachers to discuss matters of common interest will give you something to look forward to at the end of a trying day in the classroom. As you share ideas about teaching and learning, colleagues will become friends to whom you can turn for encouragement and advice. This option is open to everyone because it costs nothing but time.

PARTING THOUGHTS

Your survival in the classroom and your well-being as a person and teacher are largely up to you. Ironically, teachers are often better at telling students what to do than they are at following their own advice. Do you hear familiar echoes in the words below?

"You should be getting a much higher grade in this course. You certainly have the ability. If you would just spend a few minutes every day on your homework, you wouldn't get so far behind. And surely you knew that if you waited until the night before to begin your term project, something might come up to keep you from getting it done. Why don't you get yourself organized and plan ahead next quarter? You'll avoid a lot of hassles and get a much better grade." (What are the negative consequences when you wait until the last minute to do lesson plans or write a report for the principal?)

"Feeling sorry for yourself and complaining to your friends won't accomplish anything. Why didn't you tell me you thought I was too hard on you? I can't do anything about a situation if I don't know anything about it." (What good does it do to gripe in the teachers' room about a new directive from principal? If you tell the principal how you feel, there's a chance he might reverse himself. On the other hand, ventilating in the teachers' room may provide some temporary psychological relief, but it won't accomplish anything except perhaps to put others in a dark mood, too.)

"I can understand why you felt you needed to talk to your girl friend right away, but I still can't excuse you for missing my class. According to the school policy, that's up to the assistant principal. I have a responsibility to follow the rules myself as well as make sure you students do. Can you understand my position?" (When the principal doesn't handle a situation the way you wish she would, is it because she's prevented from doing otherwise by school board policy or a clause in the negotiated contract?)

"Of course, you can do it, but not if you think you're going to fail before you even begin. Just tackle the job one step at a time and keep telling yourself as you go along, you can do it" (How often do negative expectations cause us to give up before we even begin or create the difficult situations we'd like to avoid?)

Think about what you routinely say to students and ask yourself, "Do I practice what I preach?" You may have been providing students with solutions all along, without ever realizing how following your own advice could benefit you!

I hope this book has convinced you that lions—personal, people, and paper problems—can be tamed by organizing, planning, problem solving, looking at difficult situations from another point of view, and believing in your own power to change your life and influence similar changes in the lives of your students.

Occasionally, however, despite your very best efforts, you will come face-to-face with a stubborn lion that refuses to be tamed. When that happens consider the words of Reinhold Niebuhr:

Give me the serenity to accept the things that cannot be changed,
The courage to change the things that should be changed,
And the wisdom to know the difference.

When you tame the lions, you can transform teaching from just another way to earn a living into an exciting and challenging career.

BIBLIOGRAPHY

SMALL GROUPS IN THE CLASSROOM

Book, Cassandra and Kathleen Galvin. *Instruction in and about Small Group Discussion.* Falls Church, VA: Speech Communication Association, 1975.

Glasser, William. *Control Theory in the Classroom.* New York, NY: Harper and Row, 1986.

Hawkins, Thom. *Group Inquiry Techniques for Teaching Writing.* Urbana, IL: National Council of Teachers of English, 1976. [Good ideas for teachers of all subjects]

Johnson, David et al. *Circles of Learning: Cooperation in the Classroom.* Alexandria, VA; Association for Supervision and Curriculum Development, 1984.

Schmuck, Richard and Patricia A. Schmuck. *Group Process in the Classroom.* Dubuque, IA: Wm. C. Brown, 1973.

Stanford, Gene. *Developing Effective Classroom Groups.* New York: Hart, 1977. [Activities, including two mysteries for students to solve in groups; good information]

Stanford, Gene and Barbara Dodds Stanford. *Learning Discussion Skills Through Games.* New York: Citation Press, 1969. [Activities, including two more mysteries for students to solve in groups]

WRITING ACROSS THE CURRICULUM

Applebee, Arthur. *Writing in the Schools: English and the Content Areas.* Urbana, IL: National Council of Teachers of English, 1981.

Applebee, Arthur. *Writing in the Secondary School.* Urbana, IL: National Council of Teachers of English, 1981.

Barr, Mary et al. (Eds.). *What's Going On?* Upper Monclair, NJ: Boynton Cook, 1982. [Chapter on using writing to teach math]

Elbow, Peter, *Writing with Power.* New York: Oxford University Press, 1981.

Flower, Linda. *Problem-Solving Strategies for Writing.* New York: Harcourt Brace Jovanovich, 1981. [Good ideas for research papers]

Fulwiler, Toby and Art Young (Eds.). *Language Connections: Writing and Reading Across the Curriculum.* Urbana, IL: National Council of Teachers of English, 1982.

LeFevre, Karen and Mary Jane Dickerson. *Until I See What I Say: Teaching Writing in All Disciplines.* Montpelier, VT: IDC Publications, 1981.

Maimon, Elaine P. et al. *Writing in the Arts and Sciences*. Boston: Little Brown, 1981.

Martin, Nancy. *Writing Across the Curriculum*. Upper Montclair, NJ: Boynton Cook, 1973.

Mayher, John S. *Learning To Write/Writing to Learn*. Upper Montclair, NJ: Boynton Cook, 1983.

Myers, John W. *Writing To Learn Across the Curriculum*. Bloomington, IN: Phi Delta Kappa, 1984.

Murray, Donald M. *Learning by Teaching*. Upper Montclair, NJ: Boynton Cook, 1982.

Tchudi, Stephen and Joanne Yates. *Teaching Writing in the Content Areas: Senior High School*. Washington, DC: National Education Association, 1983. [Also another volume for junior high]

Scardamalia, Marlene et al. *Writing for Results: A Sourcebook of Consequential Composing Activities*. LaSalle, IL: Open Court, 1981. [Sixty activities described along with the subject areas where they can be used]

Walvoord, Barbara E. Fassler. *Helping Students Write Well: A Guide for Teachers in All Disciplines*. New York: Modern Language Association, 1982.

Wolfe, Denny and Robert Reising. *Writing for Learning in the Content Areas*. Portland, ME: J. Weston Walch, 1983. [Includes activities with handouts which can be copied and distributed to students as well as general information]

Yates, Joanne M. *Research Implications for Writing in the Content Areas*. Washington, DC: National Education Association, 1983.

INDEX